HAVING IT
BOTH WAYS

HAVING IT BOTH WAYS

The ABCs of Win-Win Relationships

Irwin M. Rubin, Ph.D

and

Thomas J. Campbell, M.D.

Kingsham Press

First published 2003
by Kingsham Press

Oldbury Complex
Marsh Lane
Easthampnett
Chichester, West Sussex
PO18 OJW
United Kingdom

© 2003 Irwin M. Rubin and Thomas J. Campbell

Typeset in Sabon

Printed and bound by
MPG Books
Bodmin
Cornwall
United Kingdom

ISBN: 1-904235-18-2

British Library Cataloguing in Publication Data
A catalogue record of this book is available from the British Library

Rubin, Irwin M. and Campbell, Thomas J.

Dedication

We would like to dedicate this book to you. Your commitment to creating and nurturing win-win relationships will help us all to realise a world full of people coming together to honour the right of each person to be fully who they were created to be.

Contents

Preface

A MIRACLE MOOD-ALTERING "drug" is available. The label on the side of the bottle promises, among other things, significantly enhanced personal well-being, richer relationships, and family lives, and increased organisational productivity. Additional trials will be required to determine its effect on potentially lethal conditions such as domestic violence, road rage, and murderous outbursts at work. Completely legal, and requiring no doctor's prescription, this "drug" is freely available to anyone willing to inject the win-win power of their **ABCs—A**wareness of **B**ehaviour and its **Consequences**—into any and all of their many relationships. *Having It Both Ways* will guide you in doing this.

In Chapter One, "On earth as it is in heaven", we outline our basic premise: since our Higher Power, the Universal source of goodness that surrounds us all [referred to by a variety of names—Tao, Buddha, God, Allah, Jesus, etc.—among the earth's six billion inhabitants] speaks to us through others, a daily commitment to improving the win-win quality of our day-to-day interpersonal relationships marks the path of spiritual development. A proven set of tools to help us stay on our spiritual paths is offered in Chapter Two "The **ABCs** tool kit". In Chapters Three "The proof is in the coding", and Four "Monkey see, monkey do", by analysing the interactions in familiar fairy tales, parables, and true stories, we demonstrate how using the **ABCs** tool kit contributes to creating the spiritual experiences so vital to feeding our souls. In the next chapter "What is this thing called love?", we reframe a basic biblical truth into its essential win-win terms: "Do unto others as they would have you do unto them". Several natural pitfalls that can derail us from our win-win journey are brought to light in the next chapter, "Pitfalls to be avoided".

Based on this foundation, the next several chapters—"Pregnant moments in intimate relationships"; "The gift is in the giving"; "Hello, goodbye"; and "Discourse of the silent variety"—focus on examples of the **ABCs** in action. Some conversations deal with day-to-day bread-

and-butter relationships between, for example, husbands and wives. Others, more spiritual in nature, focus on conversations we have with ourselves throughout our lives and with loved ones in the closing moments of their lives. In the chapter entitled "When you have to burn a bridge behind you", we explore how we can detect, protect, and disconnect ourselves from lose-lose co-dependent relationships.

In the final chapter, we invite the reader to join us in a "Leap of faith" as we explore the relationship between the story of the Hundredth Monkey and *Having It Both Ways*. In that relationship, as Ken Keyes has noted, "may lie our only hope of a future for our species!"

Foreword

THE LATE 20th century was a period where the focus was on the individual. This 'me' generation has pursued the satisfaction of the self, often at the expense of fellow human beings. The dawning of a new century, with its uncertainties and tensions, has brought with it a curiosity and hope for a better world. Our pursuit is now more spiritual, more sensitive to the needs of others, with a realisation that if I win and you lose, in fact, we both lose.

Having It Both Ways: The ABCs of Win-Win Relationships is not about seeking the compromise. Instead, what I learn is that to get what I want, I have to relate to you in a way that you prefer. I can value and work with our diversity, rather than hide it. We can celebrate and reap the rewards of our differences.

It's like when we dance the salsa. You and I will dance different steps, to different beats. Our effortless movements, consisting of finely balanced pushes and pulls, will flow so we appear as one. We'll attend to each other's needs and pre-empt a movement, feeling it before it happens. Each step you take means I move in a certain way. Each time I move, you will adjust your behaviour to compensate so we maintain our performance. Our salsa dance is more than the tapping out of routine steps. To be meaningful it has to have passion; my heart and your heart beating together.

Salsa dancing, when performed by two individuals who are attending to each other's movements and feelings, as well as others on the dance floor, is a beautiful activity both to watch and participate. Each step on its own is simple. It's the way in which the techniques are brought to life that creates the beauty and fluidity.

This book, *Having It Both Ways: The ABCs of Win-Win Relationships*, offers us a set of carefully crafted techniques so you and I can learn to apply music and dance to words we exchange in our relationship. We learn to code our behaviours, to see step by step how the way we choose to interact has consequences on our relationship, as well as others around us. As with any new skill, practice is important. The book provides us with a variety of contexts within which we can explore the application of new techniques. With practice, we'll learn new steps and combinations of behaviours designed to create and maintain a bond where the consequences are mutual love, comfort, and understanding.

Herman Melville reminds us that "We cannot live only for ourselves. A thousand fibres connect us with our fellow man; and among those fibres as sympathetic threads, our actions run as causes, and they come back to us as effects." The principles explained in this book will help me to unleash my potential to behave in a way that not only empowers me to treat you as you prefer, but also so I experience and get from you, the treatment that I prefer to receive.

This win-win activity is larger than the two of us. The real power in *Having It Both Ways: The ABCs of Win-Win Relationships* is the potential impact on whole communities. When we learn to dance to each other's steps we act out a universal movement whose design flows through us. Our future is created as a consequence of the choices we make in how to act. By choosing wisely and lovingly, each one of us has the opportunity to release a force for good for each one of us. Such is the power of *Having It Both Ways: The ABCs of Win-Win Relationships*.

Professor Sarah Fraser

Acknowledgements

T
HE ACKNOWLEDGEMENTS section often occupies the 'last place' position of pages to be written. Yet, the entire book could never have been completed, in the first place, without the varied contributions of many people from around the globe. These people provided many gifts; ranging from the invaluable formal editorial help provided by Wes Curry, while a new friend and colleague in Great Britain, Sarah Fraser, came on the scene to offer her support and encouragement, so vital in bringing us a publisher in the person of Anand Kumar. Over the months between the start of this book and its completion, the names of many of those people who provided invaluable comments, ideas, and suggestions found their way onto a series of yellow post-it® notes. Many, alas, but not all!

In considering how to handle this incompleteness, one option was to list the names of those we had written down—in alphabetical order, so as not to differentiate the value of a person's contribution from its extensiveness or frequency. The forgotten group would get subsumed under the category—"the many others too extensive to list". This, along with the standard disclaimer about their having no responsibility for the final product, would take care of the Acknowledgements in a traditional manner.

In the spirit of the entire book, we have chosen a different option. While the people who have contributed to this effort are different and unique in many ways, they deeply share one thing in common. They are more committed to living a set of important principles and ideals than they are to the importance of any single personality. To a person, they struggle—each in their own unique ways—to the meet the daily challenges of having it both ways.

Because you all exist in our lives, and have so generously shared your thoughts and feelings through reading earlier versions of this book, you have become a deeper part of our lives, and the lives of those who will read the final version. As a result, the possibility of Ken Keyes' hundredth monkey making itself visible is significantly enhanced.

As is the possibility of world peace.

For that gift you all have provided, we are all forever indebted and grateful.

Chapter One

On earth as it is in heaven

"I am because we are."

(African proverb)

IMAGINE SOME special moments. You're lying at the beach, mind lost in the clouds. Suddenly, a bird swoops out of the infinite blue ceiling and snaps a moth from the air just in front of your eyes. "And we think we have developed pretty sophisticated radar systems!" you muse to yourself.

Now shift your imagination from the beach up into that sky. You awaken at 35,000 feet from a few uneasy hours of shut-eye on a coast-to-coast red eye. After clearing the crusted ball of sleep stuck in the corner of your eye, the first thing you notice is a huge orange ball of fire sandwiched between two layers of jet black storm clouds. You gently shake your head to make sure you aren't dreaming. No, nature's creative power is staring you in the face.

Finally, you deplane and head back home to your family. You've been away on a trip for several weeks. As you walk through the back door, your four-year-old son leaps into your arms and throws his arms around your neck. "Daddy didn't have time to buy you a surprise to play with," you announce sheepishly. He tilts his head, purses his lips in mock chagrin, looks you straight in the eye, and responds, "I just wanna play with you, Daddy."

Experiences like these pull at the strings of your heart. A shiver runs down your spine. A tight ball begins to form in the pit of your stomach. Your tongue swipes a salty tear that has rolled down your cheek. A choked up feeling is involuntarily swallowed back.

You are absolutely certain that something special has taken place. You've never felt more fully alive, more at peace with yourself and the world. The moment is pregnant with every possibility, every dream, every hope. It's the best of the best, heaven on earth.

1

You are also aware that you, alone, didn't make it happen. The sun and the storm being in that position, the moment your eyes opened, was nothing personal. Even your son's look into your very soul, as personal as it felt, you know in your heart is a gift from a greater force beyond your self.

The six plus billion who inhabit this earth have a variety of names for this force, including among them; Tao, Buddha, Allah, Jesus, and God. Regardless of the specific label, this universal force is believed to "speak to us", reminding us of the original and continuing source of "goodness" that surrounds us all. The channel through which we hear this voice, this Higher Power, speaking to us is our soul, our Inner Self.

Except possibly for those who see them as random acts, events such as these and the feelings they generate are the essence of what most people call spiritual experiences. They serve as reminders that there resides deep within each of us that higher order goodness. When we step up to the challenge of aligning our behaviour with what we know in our hearts is right, when a Higher Power speaks to us and we listen to and act upon that voice, we feel exuberant and fully alive.

Having it Both Ways is based on the premise that our Higher Power speaks to our Inner Selves through other people. Consequently, every interaction, every relationship can be approached as if it were an opportunity to prepare the soil and sow the seeds for subsequent spiritual experiences. Every encounter with others can be looked upon as an opportunity for enlightenment—a chance for my Inner Self to speak with your Inner Self. When we can afford each other the opportunity to hear the deepest forms of love and truth echo through both of our souls, we experience the power of having it both ways.

By learning how to make use of the simple power of our **ABC**s—our **A**wareness of our **B**ehaviour and its **C**onsequences—we can increase the frequency of these moments. We will have the skills and tools to do our part in feeling at peace with ourselves and the world. We will refer to relationships in which both parties regularly feel this kind of specialness about themselves and about each other as win-win relationships.

Francis of Assisi offered us a well-recognised ideal when it comes to relationships: "Lord, grant that I may seek rather to comfort than to be comforted, to understand than to be understood, to love than to be loved; for it is in giving that we receive". We are not saints, so, in striving for this heavenly state, we will be constantly reminded of our human limitations.

At various times, our deepest selves—our hearts and souls—will also seek to receive comfort, understanding, and love. Personal dignity and self-esteem will suffer if these fundamental needs are long denied. And self-esteem—caring about and for one's self—is a precondition to caring about and for others.

These fundamental needs are God-given, our legacy at birth. Freedom rests with how we choose to satisfy them. The price for this freedom is accountability for the consequences of our choices. We can be arrogant, choosing behaviours that reflect a lack of genuine concern and responsiveness for the reality that others also need to feel comforted, understood, and loved. We can ignore the fact that we have these same needs and be martyrs, robbing ourselves of the opportunity to receive and others of the opportunity to give. We can be selfish, choosing behaviours that are aimed at meeting our own needs for comfort, understanding, and love at the expense of others.

Common belief would have us rationalise such exploitation and aggrandisement of ourselves and others as necessary evils in a world driven by a win-lose paradigm. Comfort, understanding, and love are hoarded, treated as commodities in finite and short supply. Simple economics tells us an impoverished supplier cannot meet our demands. At the same time, a spiritual axiom warns that we have to be willing to give away what we have in order to be able to keep it. In other words, I must be willing to share the comfort, understanding, and love I need to have bestowed upon me, to feel whole, in order to continue to get my own supply of these vital commodities replenished. This mutual sharing, based on the need to feed our individual Inner Selves, is the essential driving force behind the need for win-win relationships.

To further complicate matters, asking for comfort, love, and understanding is considered by many a sign of weakness. In exposing our needs by actively seeking the strengthening power of these gifts from others, we make ourselves vulnerable to rejection.

The way out of this conundrum is to embrace the fact that the more comfort, understanding, and love I can supply to you, the more you'll be able to give back to me. It may, indeed, be better to give than receive, but it must certainly be even better for both of us to give and receive.

Our global community is built upon these exchanges. We are all interconnected. Consequently, an interpersonal relationship is either a win-win—we both have it both ways—or lose-lose—neither one of us has it our way. Win-lose is a mythical outcome, for a soul not at peace with itself eventually goes to battle with others. The sage Lao-Tse portrayed this causal chain of interpersonal events this way.

"If there is to be peace in the world.
There must be peace in the nations.
If there is to be peace in the nations,
There must be peace in the cities.
If there is to be peace in the cities,
There must be peace between neighbours.
If there is to be peace between neighbours,
There must be peace in the home.
If there is to be peace in the home,
There must be peace in the heart."

In the long run, having it both ways—comforting and being comforted, understanding and being understood, loving and being loved, giving and receiving—is the only way for either of us to have our way.

Any meaningful relationship is symbiotic, a give and take of two dissimilar organisms in a close association or union that is *supposed to be advantageous to both*. Like that of Jack Sprat and his wife, our relationships with spouses, family members, work colleagues, and neighbours, to name a few, will persist only if they remain mutually beneficial, advantageous to both of us.

Nature is replete with such mutually beneficial give and take relationships. One hundred thousand times everyday—almost 3 billion times in an average lifetime—the miracle of our hearts proves the essential requirement for and power of symbiosis. Carbon dioxide is lethal to us. But the poison we exhale breathes life into plants, which need carbon dioxide for their survival. In return, they give us life-sustaining oxygen. Win-win relationships with all living beings are essential to our survival.

Whether the synergy between two people is mutually enhancing or debilitating is a function of what each person had in their hearts in the first place. This is why, for example, forgiveness and letting go of resentments become vital to our mutual well-beings. Doing so releases toxicity from our hearts. We stop beating up on ourselves, and/or the other person, for our fallible human natures. Doing so allows a more upbeat rhythm to beat into our own and others' hearts. "What comes from the heart," according to an old Polish proverb, "reaches the heart."

To ensure that we can have it both ways, that our relationships with others, beginning with ourselves, are win-win, we will need to learn to live some simple truths. Grace, humility, gratitude, and faith are among the gifts this struggle can provide. These principles are not new. They are common sense, tried and true.

Fortunately, successfully implementing these principles will not depend on our IQs alone, our brain power. The brain, seeking as it does to control, subdue, and master, follows what Riane Eilser calls the "dominator model" [1]. These are skills we will most assuredly need, for we have to be willing to heighten our conscious Awareness of our Behaviour and its Consequences. Old habits will have to be identified and subdued. New ones will have to be introduced and mastered. Doing what we know in our minds is right will also take skill power, not just will power. Atrophied behavioural muscles will have to be awakened and rejuvenated.

However, a book on relationships written solely from the brain's cognitive perspective would be akin to trying to learn to spiritually ice skate. To improve the win-win quality of our many relationships, we will also have to be willing to marshal and exercise our EQs (Emotional Intelligence)—our heart-based emotional intelligence. And the heart, according to Eisler, follows the "partnership model", which stresses respect, openness, co-operation, and harmony.

Win-win relationships require a _yes and_, not an _either or_, mind-set. The selfishness of the _me first_ generation is as unstable a basis upon which to build meaningful win-win relationships as is the idealist nature of a _you first_ mind-set. This _yes and_ model of win-win relationships, of learning to have it both ways, will require that the measured wisdom of our mature inner elder be given air time equal to the spontaneity of our innocent inner child.

Let us continue our journey by looking at a model that describes the tools available to us when we speak to each other. This model will be very biased. It will deal only with behaviours that have the potential to create win-win outcomes. Bluffing, innuendos, masked truths, pretensions—behaviours appropriate to win-lose games—will be excluded. By developing a greater Awareness of our Behaviours and their Consequences, our ABCs, we can more frequently create the conditions and opportunities that allow God to speak to and through us.

To be self'ish—to be fully the person that we were created to be—is antithetical to selfishness. This _self in the service of us_ is the essence of a true win-win relationship, of having it both ways.

Chapter Two

The ABCs tool kit

"Human beings are discourse."

(J. Rumi)

D ISCOURSE, THE communication and expression of thoughts and feelings by words and actions, is the fabric of our lives. We are constantly in relationships, either talking with other people or thinking, talking to ourselves. Knowing how the communications process between two people works is a precondition to knowing what to do to make the relationship work better. Speaking louder or tuning the other person out are as unlikely to eliminate static in a relationship as is giving the TV a good whack on the side to reduce distortion. (Indeed, both may actually increase the problem!) Knowing what to do is insufficient. We need both the right behavioural tools and the skills to use them appropriately.

The day-to-day experiences of tens of thousands of people from several cultures have gone into the creation of the tools needed to enhance our **ABCs**. We invite you to reflect on the same questions they were asked.

> Think about an interaction—more than just a chat—you had recently with someone who had the following qualities: (1) You felt good about what was accomplished (problem resolved, decision made); (2) You felt good about how you behaved; and (3) You felt good about how the other person behaved. (A win-win encounter includes these three qualities from both parties' perspectives.)
>
> Now identify an observable behaviour the other person exhibited that you feel contributed to these outcomes.

Your first responses are likely to be in the form of idealised motherhood and apple pie abstractions: good listener, honest, respectful, trustworthy. While definitely good qualities, these are not observable behaviours. A bit more probing reveals their underlying behavioural qualities. A good listener becomes someone who does not interrupt while you are speaking. An honest person becomes someone who admits mistakes.

The behaviours that repeatedly emerged are discrete and observable, and, when used appropriately and with integrity, form the ingredients for creating win-win relationships. Furthermore, the behaviours are generic, their usefulness and applicability cut across a wide variety of relationships.

A sample of these behavioural ingredients appears below in the form of a quiz designed to be completed separately by you and a significant other. You may well find your responses to be very eye-opening. (See Appendix for a detailed description of the 48 behaviours in the full win-win pool.)

Truth or consequences: a quiz

How many of the following statements can you honestly say are always true about your day-to-day behaviour towards a significant other? How many would the significant other agree are always true about your behaviour?

True or false?
- You explain the bases for your decisions?
- You tell them clearly and reasonably what you want from them?
- You tell them what you like about what they are doing?
- You admit to and apologise for your mistakes?
- You stress pulling together to achieve common goals?
- You give them the attention they need to get their points across?
- You ask questions like: "How can I help?" "How can I support you?"
- You ask them for their suggestions?
- You check understanding by paraphrasing what they have said?
- You show a genuine desire to find out how they feel?
- Now compare your responses to these questions with how your significant other responded. Notice any discrepancies.

The more two people can agree that behaviours such as these are part of their regular exchanges, the more likely they are to be having it both ways. Points of disagreement (you say True and the other says False) are normal and expected. They do not presume either person is to blame or is doing anything wrong. Rather, they point to static or distortion in the relationship between the two people. Both the sending instrument and the receiving instrument will benefit from some re-tuning and re-calibration.

But more than just words are involved. The music (our tone of voice) and the dance (our nonverbal body language) all become part of the messages we send. Our effectiveness in relationships is enhanced when our words, music, and dance are aligned. Mixed messages occur when our words speak one truth but our music and dance suggest alternative conclusions. Saying "that's a great idea" in a flat monotone while shaking your head vigorously "No way!" is an example of misaligned words music and dance. Memos, letters, and e-mails, even those with smiley faces [:-)], because they are all one-way, are consequently subject to incompleteness and misunderstanding.

In emotionally charged situations, people put more credence in a person's music and dance than they do in the person's words. A flushed red face would be more believed than a string of verbal admonitions that "I'm not embarrassed in the least!" Our minds can bend the truth, but our hearts will ache, and ultimately break, under the strain of speaking with a "forked tongue".

The ABCs tool kit provides the means that will enable us to make the adjustments and alignments necessary to develop and maintain win-win relationships. Becoming familiar with all of them will require some work. However, the return will be more than worth the investment. Effectively using the behaviours in the model will allow us to satisfy the win-win criteria referred to earlier: (1) You both will feel good about what was accomplished (problem resolved, decision made); (2) You both will feel good about how you each behaved.

The ABCs tool kit: two energy modes—push and pull

Imagine two busy people wrapped in their own thoughts, approaching an unmarked swinging door from opposite sides. They might both push or pull on the door at the same instant, thereby wasting or cancelling their energies. Indeed, some harm could occur if one delivers a hard yank at the same instant the other is putting their shoulder to the task. Ideally, they become aware of what is developing and monitor their behaviours to produce a positive consequence—in sequence, they both get through the door.

Human discourse is subject to similar challenges. We use *Push* energy in a relationship when our primary purpose is to have our thoughts and feelings better understood by another person, to get our points across to them. We use *Pull* energy when our primary purpose is to better understand another person's thoughts and feelings, to ensure we are getting the points they are trying make. A balanced use of *Push* and *Pull* allows both parties to understand and be understood so that a win-win relationship can develop.

In commenting on this dynamic, Morrie Schwartz, in *Tuesday's With Morrie* [2] by Mitch Albom (the poignant lessons on life offered by a man in his final days) referred to it as "a tension of opposites, like a pull on a rubber band ... [and] most of us live somewhere in the middle ... A series of pulls back and forth. You want to do one thing, but you are bound to do another. Something hurts you, yet you know it shouldn't. You take certain things for granted, even when you know you should never take anything for granted".

The last few lines of that "tuesday" conversation with Mitch Albom follow:

> MITCH "Sounds like a wrestling match."
> MORRIE "A wrestling match," he laughs. "Yes, I guess you could describe life that way."
> MITCH "So which side wins?"
> MORRIE "Which side wins?" Morrie smiled, through crinkled eyes and crooked teeth. "Love wins. Love always wins."

In wrestling with the challenges in our own lives, we are seeking to increase the frequency of those moments when that something special takes place. It is in those moments that we know in our hearts that our Higher Power has spoken to us, that love has won. Let us turn to specific behavioural tools that are designed to allow us to bring Morrie's prediction to life, to increase the likelihood that "love always wins".

Four Push styles: facts and feelings

Our *Push* energies, the points we try to get across in any relationship, fall into one of four categories: Describe, Prescribe, Appreciate, and Inspire.

Describe and Prescribe: when the facts are the heart of the matter

Describes are characterised by crisp data, logic, and facts to explain, debate, justify a position or idea. *Because of ...* and *The reasons why ...*

are typical sentence stems associated with Describes. In response to the question *What time is it?* We should offer a simple fact, *It's 3:00 p.m.*

Sherlock Holmes was logic personified—*Just the facts Watson, just the facts*. His music was level, unheated, without inflection or rhythm. Nary a smile disturbed the stoic nature of his dance. Mr. Spock played a similar role on the Starship Enterprise—a human computer, devoid of the troublesome influence of feelings, preferences, and needs on important decisions. Indeed, when someone is trying to argue a point and gets hot under the collar, efforts are made to help that person stay cool, to get a hold of their feelings.

Prescribes are characterised by rational, clear, unambiguous thoughts and ideas as to what ought to, should be, or must become true in the future—*My suggestion is ..., I propose ..., I need ....* We want our reasonable and logical proposals and suggestions as well as our descriptive factual justifications for them to be fully understood.

Rhythm and dance steps take on a different tone. Confidence in one's own proposal carries more weight than hesitancy. *Ers* and negative qualifiers are to be avoided—*You probably won't like this idea but ...* Fingers focus attention—*I'll take that one.* Voice tone is unwavering but not shouting. Shoulders are erect with assertiveness, not pulled back in arrogance. Whining and pleading have no place.

Prescribe and Describe fit together like a hand in a glove:

- My suggestion is that we go with Supplier X (*Prescribe*) because its prices are 15% lower than those of its nearest competitor. (*Describe*)
- I propose we visit my folks this Xmas. (*Prescribe*) We've visited yours twice in row now. (*Describe*)
- I need some help with the dishes. (*Prescribe*) I'm running behind for my meeting. (*Describe*)
- I've out-sold everyone else two years running. (*Describe*) I deserve at least a ten percent raise. (*Prescribe*)

However, making sure the facts of the matter on our minds are understood is not all that matters to us. What we honestly feel in our hearts also matters.

Appreciate and Inspire: when the facts aren't all that matters

Appreciates are characterised by the feelings I have about what you have done or said. The praise and constructive criticism at its core, spoken honestly and with compassion, form the basis for the feedback that is the breakfast of champions—*I like ..., I dislike ....* Apologising sincerely for mistakes *(I'm sorry)* and saying *Thank you* are also powerful acts of appreciation.

Indeed, words of appreciation such as *Thank you* or *I'm sorry*, when spoken from the heart, can wipe away a lifetime of pain, as W.H. Hudson [3] wrote in his autobiography of his schoolboy experiences. After a falling out with a friend, they avoided each other. "Boys are always inarticulate," Hudson noted, "where their deepest feelings are concerned; they cannot express kind and sympathetic feelings." Hudson recalls that one day, "He all at once came up to me and holding out his hand said, 'Let's be friends.' I was more grateful to him than I have ever felt towards anyone since, just because by his approaching me first [and apologising], I was spared the agony of having to say 'I'm sorry' first. It took him all his courage to speak those three simple words."

Inspires are characterised by the dreams, hopes, and visions harboured in our hearts of what could become true in the future. Faith and passion, not data and logic, fuel our efforts to *Push* our deepest feelings across to someone. *Imagine how incredible it will feel when they drape that gold medal across your neck!* Painting such vivid pictures and other efforts to evoke or enthuse someone to join with us *(Together we can walk where no man has gone before!)* in sharing a heartfelt feeling or in achieving some future-oriented goal are the core of our Inspires.

Both Prescribes and Inspires are attempts to *Push* a particular point about the future across to someone. In the case of a Prescribe, the challenge is to be crisp and clear and to use the minimum number of rationalising words so not to waffle. When we Inspire, on the other hand, we strive to remember that a single picture is worth a thousand words. Martin Luther King, Jr. began his famous speech with a heartfelt dream, not a detailed list of rational proposals and a flood of facts supporting the wrongness of racism.

In varying combinations, all of these *Push* behaviours are vital tools in ensuring that my needs for comfort, understanding, and love are understood. *It disappoints me when you don't let me finish speaking,* an owned behavioural Appreciate feedback, is dramatically different from *You are insensitive*, a personality attribution. Similarly, *I need you to not interrupt me*, an owned Prescribe, is dramatically different from *You shouldn't be so controlling*, an ascription of blame. My accountability and choice is in the words, music, and dance of how I voice these needs. Whether or not you decide to meet them is your choice and accountability.

When we are striving to communicate aspects of our total beings, to give full voice to our hearts and our minds, we use our energy to *Push*. *Push* energy provides a vehicle for us to express our Inner Self—to Describe our thoughts, to Prescribe our wants and needs, to Appreciate our feelings and judgements, and to Inspire from our souls to keep striving for visions and dreams. The four *Push* options are summarised on the upper half of the ABCs Behavioural Compass. (See Figure 1.)

Because Describe and Prescribe are fact-oriented styles, they are positioned towards the relative coolness of the North Pole. Appreciate and Inspire, consistent with their emotion-oriented natures, are positioned closer to the warmth of the Equator. Let us now turn to the lower hemisphere, which contains the four *Pull* behavioural styles: Attend, Ask, Understand, and Empathise.

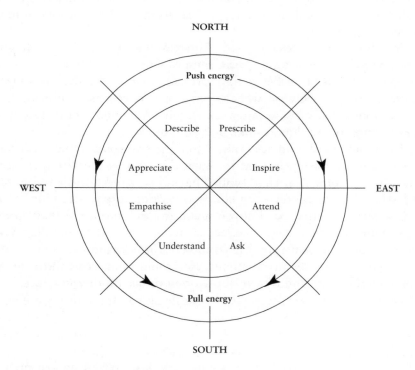

Figure 1 ABCs behavioural compass

Four Pull styles

In striving to be sure we understand, we are, in effect, doing what we can to enable the other person to feel understood by us and by themselves. We are helping them to formulate and then *Push* their ideas, thoughts, feelings, and dreams across to us. Together, *Push* and *Pull* form the yin and yang of win-win relationships.

Attend

On the surface, the first thing we must do is deceptively simple and completely nonverbal. We must close our mouths and not fiddle with any papers, take any phone calls, or sneak glances at the sports scores on the TV set in the background. That's the easy part. The hard part is to quiet the endless chatter going on in our minds, when painted smiles and mechanical head nods are masking rehearsals of your own next salvo of *Push*es, judgements, and rebuttals. By making ourselves physically and emotionally receptive, we can Attend, a prerequisite to more active *Pull*ing.

In talking one "tuesday" with Mitch Albom about "how love goes on", Morrie Schwartz put great emphasis on the "pulling" power of Attend—"I believe in being fully present ... *with* the person you are with ... focused only on what's going on between us ... not thinking about something we said last week ... what's coming up this Friday ... I'm talking to you. I am thinking about you."

Upon hearing this advice on how to keep love going, Mitch reflected, "I remembered how he used to teach this idea in the Group Process class back at Brandies. I had scoffed back then, thinking this was hardly a lesson plan for a university course. Learning to pay attention? How important could that be? I now know it is more important than almost everything they taught us in college ... We are great at small talk: 'What do you do?' 'Where do you live?' But *really* listening to someone—without trying to sell them something, pick them up, recruit them, or get some kind of status in return—how often do we do this anymore?"

Perhaps the greatest present we can exchange is the gift of our presence.

Ask

Having made ourselves alert to whatever is unfolding in the present moment, we can now proceed to more actively help the other person express his or her thoughts, feelings, dreams, or ideas. When we would sincerely like to encourage others to get their points across to us, we can

Pull and Ask. Doing so enables us to understand them, and makes them feel understood—having it both ways. Using open-ended, non-judgmental questions, we can invite the other person to Describe *(Can you help me understand why that's so important?)*, Prescribe *(What is it exactly you'd like me to do to help?)*, Appreciate *(How do you feel about the report I wrote?)*, and/or Inspire *(What is your fondest hope about what we might accomplish?)*.

By our use of Attend and Ask, we have primed the conversational pump. If we sincerely desire to keep the flow going, or more precisely, coming towards us from the other person, we must be careful not to stem the tide. Vigorous head nods saying *No* and verbal *Yeah, buts ...*, all examples of *Push* behaviours, must be studiously avoided. In addition to continuing to patiently Attend and Ask, we can encourage the other person to continue, and thereby broaden and deepen the relationship, by using two reflective mirrors.

Understand and Empathise: active reflection

By paraphrasing the logical essence of what has been Pushed towards us *(So, what you're telling me is if I do the dishes periodically, you'll feel as if I really care. So, in other words, if I agree to visit your folks this Christmas, you'll feel less torn.)*, we actively demonstrate that the message sent has been received. Rather than simply saying, "I understand," we demonstrate, verbally and nonverbally that we have, in fact, got the facts of the matter from the other person's point of view. We Understand.

But what if the other person is *Push*ing their feelings about a matter, not just the facts that matter to them? When a person is struggling to express feelings (including any about themselves, another person, us, and/or their dreams and hopes), they are disclosing vulnerable parts of themselves. The utmost of care must be exhibited, for these feelings are like the first sparks of fire to emerge from an effort to rub two sticks together. Any gales of wind, any *Push* back *(Hey, you're a big boy! You can handle it! Aren't you making a mountain out of a molehill?)* can dampen the other's spirit to continue and may even put the flame of desire out completely *(You're right. It's no big deal.)*.

When a person ventures forth with a feeling, and it is our intention to be a partner in a win-win relationship, we must use the second of our reflective mirrors. We Empathise by reflecting back emotional feelings in contrast to rational facts *(You sound like you're upset with me .... You must have been on cloud nine when she .... I can imagine how frightening it must have felt to ...)*.

To Understand or to Empathise is distinct from agreeing. To resonate with how another person is feeling (walking a mile in the person's shoes) is not the same as owning the same feeling ourselves, having walked a similar mile in our own shoes. The latter reflects sympathy, while the former reflects empathy.

Similarly, simply because I now understand your thoughts and feelings does not necessarily mean I agree with them. My agreement, or lack thereof, will be communicated when I stop *Pull*ing and *Push* back. Indeed, to agree or disagree with someone prior to demonstrating that I understand their point of view is to expose my prejudices and risk closing off further communication.

When all the points on our **ABCs** Behavioural Compass (Figure 1) are working in harmony, the behavioural qualities essential to a win-win state of being develop. To rise to this challenge, Leo Buscaglia notes [4], is daunting, for it demands that "you want to give the best you there is. And that means developing all the wonder of you … as a unique human being". He goes on to point out that the potential rewards for two people being willing to make such an investment in one another matches the price: "I find [such] love like a mirror. When I love another, [s]he becomes my mirror and I become [hers] his, and reflecting in each other's love we see infinity."

By individually doing what you and I can to help each other—us—understand and be understood by each other, we are acting in the self-'ish manner described earlier. If the wrestling match of life is approached as a win-win, we can both strengthen our *Push* and *Pull* muscles. Consequently, we are not only getting our individual needs met, we are, at the same time, increasing our ability to help ourselves, and the other, continue to get our respective needs met.

It is this *yes and* accountability that results in win-win relationships—loving and being loved, comforting and being comforted, understanding and being understood. What is required is a willingness, desire, and ability on my part to contribute what I can to satisfying my needs *and* yours, to ensuring my joy *and* your joy. In win-win relationships, both parties can agree to the following: *I will struggle to learn how to identify, voice, and negotiate for the satisfaction of my needs **and** do what I can to help you do the same.*

In sharing his wisdom about *How To Live With Another Person*, Viscott [5] puts it this way: "To love and be loved is to feel the sun from both sides."

This *self in the service of us* is the essence of a true win-win relationship, of having it both ways.

Chapter Three

The proof is in the coding

W E PROMISED a reward for investing in becoming familiar with the behaviours in the **ABCs** tool kit: the ability to fashion more moments where you are absolutely certain that *something special* has taken place. Let us test that promise by returning to "your four-year-old son." Because the only gift he really wanted was to play with you, you've made a special effort to read him the bedtime story he's missed from you the past several weeks.

Surrounded by teddy bears and jungle animals, he pats the side of his bed in anxious anticipation. You'd love to select a new unread story, so you could skip a few lines and hit the sack yourself. Pinocchio, his current favourite, which he has committed to memory, is in his hands.

"The part about his nose, Daddy! Read—me that part!" he squeals. As you read the accounting of Pinocchio's telling mistruths and the effect it had on the size of his nose, you can see your son's mind working at full speed. As you close the book, your son sits up, rubs his nose, and says, "See Daddy, I didn't tell any fibs today!"

Imbedded in children's stories, through the power of allegory, are vital reminders about what is right versus wrong, what is good versus bad. The moral of the story or parable conveys markers guiding the day-to-day behavioural choices that will keep us walking on the spiritual path of truth.

As adults, reading a particularly powerful story or seeing an emotional movie can result in the experience of a deep feeling: A shiver runs down your spine. *A tight ball begins to form in the pit of your stomach. Your tongue swipes the salty tear that has rolled down your cheek.* We feel a renewed sense of commitment to live a truth we have known all along. We make a silent promise to our Inner Self, to our souls, to in some way be better persons.

Familiarisation with the behaviours available in the **ABCs** tool kit will help us see *how* the characters in the story or movie behaved towards one another to create the outcome that left us feeling *something special*. What combination of *Push* and *Pull* energies were used?

How did each of the four *Push* and *Pull* styles of communicating (tools that the author of the story or parable, unfamiliar with the ABCs, presumably used naturally) contribute to the learning, or in the case of adults, relearning, of some fundamental truth or lesson about the right way to conduct ourselves? If we can gain a measure of learning *how* it came out right, in addition to the reminder as to *what* is *right*, we can use this knowledge to increase our own **ABCs**. In our day-to-day relationships, we can, with greater **A**wareness, consciously choose **B**ehaviours more likely to replicate this something special as a **C**onsequence.

The skill of coding

In exploring the **ABCs** Tool Kit, you have already experienced the process used to shed insight on the question of how. In demonstrating how some of the *Push* styles fit together, one of the examples offered was: *I need some help with the dishes.* (Prescribe) *I'm running behind for my meeting.* (Describe) The parenthesised style label signifies that the first sentence is an example of *Push* energy used to Prescribe. The second sentence is an example of *Push* energy used to Describe. (Again, a full description of all of the 48 behaviours that make up the eight *Push* and *Pull* styles is contained in the Appendix. A detailed understanding of all of them is, however, not a prerequisite to benefiting from what follows.)

Coding is the process of identifying a statement as being reflective of one of the specific *Push* or *Pull* styles. To achieve a desired outcome, we need to distinguish a Describe from a Prescribe, an Understand from an Empathise.

When is losing winning?

Professional sports have become a dominant force shaping our values and ideals. Defensive gladiators swathed in pads and helmets get enormous performance bonuses every time they smash an opposing quarterback to the ground. Their counterparts on skates draw standing ovations from bloodthirsty home crowds when a visiting player is crushed into the boards. Batters are forced to the dirt to avoid being hit by a baseball travelling at 100 miles per hour.

Show me a good loser and I'll show you a loser is the byline in a world driven by a win-lose paradigm where comfort, understanding, and love are hoarded, treated as commodities in finite and short supply. Alongside this obsession with competition and winning, we have to wonder about the viability of another old adage, *It's not whether you win or lose, but how you play the game.*

Even in the face of the agony of defeat, can we find it in our hearts to allow human concerns to rise above the thrill of victory? Can we sacrifice the impermanent fading glitter of a gold medal around our necks for a taste of the everlasting power of humility? Can embracing a willingness to lose at one game lead to our becoming winners in an even bigger game?

In resounding fashion, the true story that follows below [6] answers *YES!* to each of these challenges. The real power of the story comes from the actions described. The key win-win messages are provided by music and dance as distinct from the words. Several examples of non-verbal behaviours reflective of Inspire, Appreciate, Empathy, and Understanding will be highlighted. Actions do speak louder than words.

Chush is a school in Brooklyn, New York that caters to learning-disabled children. Some children remain in Chush for their entire school careers, while others can be mainstreamed into conventional Jewish schools.

At a Chush fund-raising dinner, the father of a Chush child delivered a speech that would never be forgotten by all who attended. After extolling the school and its dedicated staff, he cried out, "Where is the perfection in my son Shaya? Everything that God does is done with perfection. But my child cannot understand things as other children do. My child cannot remember facts and figures as other children do. Where is God's perfection?"

The audience was shocked by the question, pained by the father's anguish, and stilled by his piercing query.

"I believe," the father answered, "that when God brings a child like this into the world, the perfection that He seeks is in the way people react to this child." He then told the following story about his son Shaya.

Shaya attends Chush throughout the week and a boys' yeshiva (Torah institute) on Sundays. One Sunday afternoon, Shaya and his father came to the yeshiva as his classmates were playing baseball. The game was in progress and as Shaya and his father made their way towards the ball field, Shaya said, "Do you think you could get me into the game?"

Shaya's father knew his son was not at all athletic and that most boys would not want him on their team. But Shaya's father understood that if his son was chosen, it would give him a comfortable feeling of belonging.

Shaya's father approached one of the boys in the field and asked, "Do you think my Shaya could get into the game?"

The boy looked around for guidance from his team-mates. Getting none, he took matters into his own hands and said, "We are losing by six runs and the game is already in the eighth inning. I guess he can be on our team, and we'll try to put him up to bat in the ninth inning."

Shaya's father was ecstatic as Shaya smiled broadly. Shaya was told to put on a glove and go out to play short centre field.

In the bottom of the eight inning, Shaya's team scored a few runs but was still behind by three. In the bottom of the ninth inning, Shaya's team scored again, and now with two outs and the bases loaded and the potential winning runs on base, Shaya was scheduled to be up. Would the team actually let Shaya bat at this juncture and give away their chance to win the game?

Let us stop for a moment and reflect upon what we see emerging thus far. A loving father's efforts to give his son a moment of joy by *Ask*ing on his son's behalf, "Do you think my Shaya could get into the game?" comes as no surprise. We expect mature adults to feel ecstatic when one of their children has reason to smile broadly. But we are also reminded that significant acts of unselfish compassionate leadership are not age dependent. The young boy, who got no guidance from his team-mates as to how to handle this significant moment, "took matters into his own hands". His *Describe* logically rationalised a difficult choice: "We are losing by six runs and the game is already in the eighth inning".

The young boy probably never heard of Edward Everett Hale but he certainly lived Hale's message: "I am only one, but I am still one. I cannot do everything, but I can still do something. And, because I cannot do everything, I will not refuse to do the something that I can". Standing alone with the spectre of potential ridicule from his own peers hanging over his head, he opened a door and allowed a ray of sunshine and hope to bathe Shaya's soul. He followed his heart. Is there a simpler definition of what it takes to *Inspire* as a leader than a vision and the courage to follow it, in spite of other's judgments?

Before we continue the story, take a moment and reflect upon the various outcomes imaginable. Consider the consequences of these outcomes upon Shaya, his team, the opposing team and the parents and children watching the game.

Surprisingly, Shaya was told to take a bat and try to get a hit. Everyone knew that it was all but impossible, for Shaya didn't even know how to hold the bat properly, let alone hit with it. However, as Shaya stepped up to the plate, the pitcher moved in a few steps to lob the ball in softly so Shaya would at least be able to make contact.

The first pitch came in and Shaya swung clumsily and missed. One of Shaya's team-mates came up to Shaya and, together, they held the bat and faced the pitcher waiting for the next pitch. The pitcher again took a few steps forward to toss the ball softly to Shaya.

As the next pitch came in, Shaya and his team-mate swung the bat and together they hit a slow ground ball to the pitcher. The pitcher picked up the soft grounder and could easily have thrown the ball to the first baseman, and that would have ended the game.

Instead, the pitcher took the ball and threw it on a high arc to right field, far and wide beyond the first baseman's reach. Everyone started yelling, "Shaya, run to first! Shaya run to first!" Never in his life had Shaya run to first.

He scampered down the baseline wide-eyed and startled. By the time he reached first base, the right fielder had the ball. He could have thrown the ball to the second baseman who could tag out Shaya, who was still running. But the right fielder understood what the pitcher's intentions were, so he threw the ball high and far over the third baseman's head, as everyone yelled, "Shaya, run to second! Shaya, run to second!"

When Shaya's team-mate "came up to Shaya and, together, they held the bat" we are given an example of the power of *Inspire* in action. Acting together, we can do what one of us alone could not accomplish. This behaviour comes on the heels of an act of *Empathy*, an act of personal leadership: "the pitcher moved in a few steps to lob the ball in softly so Shaya would at least be able to make contact." Furthermore, rather than compensating for the help Shaya was getting from the team-mate holding the bat by moving back or increasing the speed of his pitch, the pitcher "again took a few steps forward."

Appreciate, Empathise, and Inspire have the power to push others to heights they never knew existed, to encourage them to do more than they thought was possible. In other words, they are highly infectious. Consequently, the right fielder could *Understand* "what the pitcher's intentions were" and he, like everyone who yelled, got caught up in the powerful slip-stream of a dream taking shape.

The infectious power of *Inspire* spreads even further as we shall see below when "the boys from both teams", themselves now also delirious with ecstasy, meet on the common ground of getting Shaya home. And, when he gets there, "all 18 boys lifted him on their shoulders and made him the hero".

Shaya ran towards second base as the runners ahead of him deliriously circled the bases towards home. As Shaya reached second base, the opposing short stop ran towards him, turned him towards the direction of third base and shouted, "Shaya, run to third!"

As Shaya rounded third, the boys from both teams ran behind him screaming, "Shaya, run home! Shaya, run home!"

Shaya ran home, stepped on home plate and all 18 boys lifted him on their shoulders and made him the hero, as he had just hit the "grand slam" and won the game for his team.

"That day," said the father who now had tears rolling down his face, "those 18 boys reached their level of perfection. They showed that it is not only those with recognised talent who should be recognised but also those who have less talent. They too are human beings, they too have feelings and emotions, they too are people, they too want to feel important."

Any serious athlete knows they can improve their game by playing against someone who is physically stronger and more skilled. By doing so, even though they are not likely to win the game very often, their physical muscles and game skills will be honed more sharply. Shaya had fewer of the physical gifts to offer than his team-mates enjoyed. As a result of his being physically challenged, he had a well-developed set of emotionally-related gifts. He offered the hope that playing a game against someone spiritually stronger might allow us to strengthen those same muscles within ourselves.

Shaya was a hero, not because he had actually "just hit a 'grand slam.'" He was a hero because he brought every one of his team-mates (not to mention those in the stands ... and we, as readers) in touch with the best of ourselves. The central source of all the heroes that lay dormant in us is in our souls, in our Inner Selves. Little wonder the story yields that something special we know means a Higher Power has spoken to us through others.

While our egos often voraciously feed upon other's losses, our souls cry deeply over the agony of defeat. In the game of life, our souls thirst for the thrill of victory. But this thirst will only be satisfied by the adrenalin rush we get from finding unique and creative ways to collaborate, from finding ways of having it both ways.

A host of nice outcomes was possible. Shaya's team-mates could have pinch hit for him. The opposition, having given Shaya his moment in the sun, could have thrown him out and still won the game. Everyone involved would have felt better, to some degree, as a result of such generosity and compassion. But when the best of us is given full rein, when the "goodness" of our Inner Selves is given full voice, what we are capable of seems almost magical.

In reaching "their level of perfection," these 18 boys remind us, Shaya's father *Describes*, that "those who have less talent ... too are human beings, they too have feelings and emotions, they too are people, they too want to feel important", just like us.

Chapter Four

Monkey see, monkey do

R EADING ABOUT Shaya, or children's stories such as Pinocchio, can plant the seeds of vital truths into growing minds and hearts. But these seeds will wither and die if the day-to-day feeding and nurturing they receive in the form of our own adult behaviour conveys an opposing message.

Suppose that after our hypothetical son rubbed his own nose and said, "See Daddy, I didn't tell any fibs today!" he then asked, "Did your nose ever get big, Daddy?" As the options available to the father flash across the screen of his mind, he may even unconsciously reach up and scratch his nose!

However the conversation unfolds, the moment is pregnant with all kinds of possibilities for teaching a young heart some painful truths and for deepening the bonding between a father and son. One would hope it begins with a humble admission of a mistake, a *Describe*, "Yes son, Daddy has told fibs before". And, to relieve his son's anxious heart, a *Prescribe* would be in order: "If I tell a fib, my nose doesn't get bigger but my heart feels bad".

The next two stories—one a familiar children's story we've read and passed on to our own children and one a true story about a teacher— will speak to the power of mimicry in learning our **ABCs**. Early social- isation experiences can be powerful in either dampening or amplifying our future success and happiness.

The negative roots run deep

Let us begin with the story of Bambi [7], an example of the kind of not- so-positive dynamics set in motion when parents, teachers and other authority figures lack the skills and abilities needed to model win-win relationships with young children.

In his early "teenage" years, Bambi found himself in love with Faline. As they walked softly side by side through the forest, quietly building their future lives together, they were interrupted by nearby rustling sounds. The last time Bambi had seen the old stag, who was now ignoring him while feasting on grass, was when Bambi was just learning to stand on his own feet. The gigantic grey shadow that spilled over their tanned coats drew an involuntary cry from Faline while Bambi choked in fear. His need to protect his loved one was strong. He also felt excitement and admiration for his magnificent father. It was as if he was mystically viewing a replica of his own destiny.

Spurred by the silent tongue lashing he was giving himself for feeling so timid, Bambi announced to Faline "It's perfectly absurd. I'm going straight over to tell him who I am."

Faline, sharing neither Bambi's courage nor his complex Oedipal needs, ran off crying and thus avoided the impending confrontation. Except for his pride, and the fact that the stag's eyes locked on his for a second before gazing haughtily off into space again, Bambi would gladly have followed her. Heart pounding, Bambi moved forward.

The ensuing passages paint a vivid picture of the *authoritative* early roots that nourish our fears of speaking what in our hearts and minds we know to be the truth. These passages are particularly poignant in giving us a glimpse of what was being thought and felt but not spoken. Therefore, we can reflect upon the inner peace father and son might have experienced if they had spoken their pieces.

> Bambi did not know what to do. He had come with the firm intention of speaking to the stag. He wanted to say, "Good day, I am Bambi. May I ask to know your honourable name also?"
>
> Yes, it had all seemed very easy, but now it appeared that the affair was not so simple. What good were the best of intentions now? Bambi did not want to seem ill-bred, as he would be if he went off without saying a word. But he did not want to seem forward either, as he would if he began the conversation.

One of the roots of failed win-win relationships is visible in the form of things we were taught about being on good behaviour. Bambi, like many of us, heard many Prescribes telling him it was impolite to seem forward by initiating conversations with elders. Respecting your elders meant, "Speak only when spoken to". On the other hand, he was also taught that it would make others think he was ill bred if he walked by someone he recognised without acknowledging in some way their meeting. As we shall see, such mixed Prescribe messages can wreak havoc when it comes to win-win outcomes. Little wonder Bambi did not know what to do, in spite of his firm intention. As our fairy tale forewarns us, the consequences of feeling unable to act on the heartfelt intentions emanating from our Inner selves are sad indeed.

The stag was wonderfully majestic. It delighted Bambi and made him feel humble. He tried in vain to arouse his courage and kept asking himself, "Why do I let him frighten me? Am I not as good as he is?" But it was no use. Bambi continued to be frightened and felt in his heart of hearts that he really was not as good as the old stag. Far from it. He felt wretched and had to use all his strength to keep himself steady.

The old stag looked at Bambi and thought "He's so charming, so delicate, so poised, so elegant in his whole bearing. I must not stare at him though. It really isn't the thing to do. Besides it might embarrass him." So he stared over Bambi's head into the empty air again.

"What a haughty look," thought Bambi. "It's unbearable, the opinion such people have of themselves."

The stag was thinking "I'd like to talk to him, he looks so sympathetic. How stupid never to speak to people we don't know." He looked thoughtfully ahead of him.

"I might as well be air," said Bambi to himself. "This fellow acts as though he were the only thing on the face of the earth."

"What should I say to him?" the old stag was wondering. "I'm not used to talking. I'd say something stupid and make myself look ridiculous ... for he's undoubtedly clever."

Bambi pulled himself together and looked fixedly at the stag. "How splendid he is," he thought despairingly.

"Well some other time, perhaps," the stag decided and walked off, dissatisfied but majestic.

Bambi remained filled with bitterness.

Familiar rationalisations (*I'm not used to talking. I'd say something stupid and make myself look ridiculous. Besides it might embarrass him.*) are examples of *Push Describes*. They allow our logical minds (our IQs) to talk ourselves out of doing what our hearts (our EQs) know is the right thing to do. The result of such inconsistency cuts deeply. In this case, two *Appreciates* never got expressed. Bambi didn't hear that his father felt Bambi was *so charming, so delicate, so poised, so elegant in his whole bearing.* And, the old stag was robbed of the joy of knowing that in the eyes of a loved one, *How splendid ... and wonderfully majestic he is.*

The stag's self-awareness of *How stupid [it is] to never speak to people we don't know* was not strong enough to overcome his pride. Our egos are masters at hiding opportunities for growth. The absence of effective feedback [8], of a reflective mirror into his own soul, would leave the stag moving through his twilight years carrying the unhealed wounds of these scars, *majestic but dissatisfied.*

For his part, Bambi would not only inherit the stag's majesty, but many of the same unhealthy thoughts. If Bambi were fortunate, someone else might have the courage and skills to help him to see and accept his *handsome … charming … delicate … poised … elegant bearing*. Because of his father's inability to voice these Appreciates, Bambi's heart was robbed of the lasting joy of feeling loved. Bambi would crave that boost to his self-esteem to heal his *bitterness* and assuage the feeling in *his heart of hearts that he was not really as good as the old stag*.

The power of fairy tales is that they enable us to see and accept the painfully clear real life consequences of a lack of tools for having it both ways. As a result of their own authoritative roots, many parents grow into their twilight years feeling *majestic but dissatisfied* without feeling comforted, understood, and loved. Often, their children nurse a deep sense of *bitterness* and damaged self-esteem scarred by a scarcity of comfort, understanding, and love. These children will someday become parents who face the same challenge, and the beat goes on. Instead of having it both ways, neither one understands or feels understood by the other. Neither has it either way.

Positive seeds can be planted

It doesn't have to be that way. In our early years, caring authoritative figures can instil a more positive attitude towards speaking from our hearts. The following true story documents how seeds can be planted that will nourish our self-esteem for many years to come. (The story, which appeared on the Internet, was originally written by Sister Helen P. Mrosla, edited and paraphrased for use.)

He was in the first third grade class I taught at Saint Mary's School in Morris, Minnesota. All 34 of my students were dear to me, but Mark Eklund was one in a million. Very neat in appearance, he had that happy-to-be-alive attitude that made even his occasional mischievousness delightful. Mark talked incessantly. I had to remind him again and again that talking without permission was not acceptable. What impressed me so much, though, was his sincere response every time I had to correct him for misbehaving—"Thank you for correcting me, Sister!" I didn't know what to make of it at first, but before long I became accustomed to hearing it many times a day.

One morning my patience was growing thin when Mark talked once too often, and then I made a novice-teacher mistake. I looked at Mark and said, "If you say one more word, I am going to tape your mouth shut!" It wasn't ten seconds later when Chuck blurted out, "Mark is talking again." I hadn't asked any of the students to help me watch Mark, but since I had stated the punishment in front of the class, I had to act on it. I remember the scene as if it had occurred this morning. I walked to my desk, very deliberately opened my drawer and took out a roll of masking tape. Without saying a word, I proceeded to Mark's desk, tore off two pieces of tape and made a big X with them over his mouth. I then returned to the front of the room. As I glanced at Mark to see how he was doing, he winked at me. That did it!! I started laughing. The class cheered as I walked back to Mark's desk, removed the tape, and shrugged my shoulders. His first words were "Thank you for correcting me, Sister."

Sister Mrosla admits to having made one novice-teacher's mistake. As soon as she *Prescribed, If you say one more word, I'm going to tape your mouth shut,* Sister Mrosla wished she hadn't opened hers! She reminds us that we need to think a moment about our contingent Prescribes—"If you do xxxx, then I will do yyyy!" Impulsive Prescribes seldom contribute to win-win outcomes. In this case, Sister Mrosla felt foolish. Her integrity was on the line. She had to act and tape a big X to mark the spot.

We think she also made another very common mistake. Mark's *sincere response every time [she] had to correct him for misbehaving—"Thank you for correcting me, Sister!"* were words of *Appreciation.* But Mark's music and dance did not match his words. Apologies lose their sincerity quickly when not followed by different behaviour. Indeed, the most meaningful apology we can ever make is to not repeat the behaviour that caused the need for it in the first place!

But Sister Mrosla more than made up for these human foibles. In the single act of laughing aloud at herself, she both *Describes*—by admitting her mistake—and *Appreciates*—by apologising for it. In so doing, she did not weaken her authority, as many would often fear. Quite the contrary, by showing her humility—owning her hubris—she reinforced her humanness. Her authoritative power, as we shall see as her story continues, increased rather than decreased.

At the end of the year, I was asked to teach junior high math. The years flew by, and before I knew it, Mark was in my classroom again. He was more handsome than ever and just as polite. Since he had to listen carefully to my instruction in the "new math", he did not talk as much in ninth grade as he had in third. One Friday, things just didn't feel right. We had worked hard on a new concept all week, and I sensed that the students were frowning, frustrated with themselves, and edgy with one another. I had to stop this crankiness before it got out of hand. So I asked them to list the names of the other students in the room on two sheets of paper, leaving a space between each name. Then I told them to think of the nicest thing they could say about each of their classmates and write it.

It took the remainder of the class period to finish their assignment, and, as the students left the room, each one handed me the papers. Charlie smiled. Mark said "Thank you for teaching me, Sister. Have a good weekend."

That Saturday, I wrote down the name of each student on separate sheets of paper, and I listed what everyone else had said about that individual. On Monday, I gave each student his or her list. Before long, the entire class was smiling. "Really?" I heard whispered. "I never knew that meant anything to anyone!" "I didn't know others like me so much." No one ever mentioned those papers in class again. I never knew if they discussed them after class or with their parents, but it didn't matter. The exercise had accomplished its purpose. The students were happy with themselves and one another again. That group of students moved on.

In this passage, Sister Mrosla provides us with several invaluable lessons in the use of our **ABCs**. When her students *were frowning, frustrated with themselves, and edgy with one another,* any number of *Prescribes* could have been used such as, "Stop all this fussing". An *Empathy* might have been thrown in as well: "I know how hard it is to learn a new concept, but just settle down!" These statements or others like them would probably have stopped the *crankiness before it got out of hand,* but would have left the cause of the crankiness untouched. The students were feeling badly about themselves and projecting some of that upset feeling upon their classmates. So, what Sister Mrosla *Prescribed* was a task that forced the students to express their *Appreciation* of one another: *I told them to think of the nicest thing they could say about each of their classmates and write it.* In so doing, she gave them the opportunity to, once again, feel *happy with themselves and one another.*

Furthermore, she not only Prescribed that they do it, she walked her own talk by participating with them. She took the time on her days off to collate all the data and *listed what everyone else had said about [an] individual.* Their pleasant whispered surprises (*I didn't know others like me so much. I never knew that meant anything to anyone.*) confirmed her hunch. It was the strings of their hearts that needed some pulling, not leashes around their necks.

As the story closes, we can compare the long-term consequences of the pregnant moments Sister Mrosla's students experienced with Bambi's need to boost his self-esteem to heal his *bitterness* and assuage the feeling in *his heart of hearts that he was not really as good as the old stag.* While the old stag was robbed of the joy of knowing that, in the eyes of a loved one, *How splendid ... and wonderfully majestic he is,* Sister Mrosla's reminder was quite the opposite.

Several years later, after I returned from vacation, I was shocked to find out Mark had been killed in Vietnam and was being buried tomorrow. His parents had asked if I could attend.

I had never seen a serviceman in a military coffin before. Mark looked so handsome, so mature. All I could think at the moment was "Mark, I would give all the masking tape in the world if only you could talk to me." I was the last one to bless the coffin. As I stood there, one of the soldiers who acted as pallbearer came up to me. "Were you Mark's math teacher?" he asked. I nodded as I continued to stare at the coffin. "Mark talked about you a lot," he said.

After the funeral, most of Mark's former classmates headed to Chuck's farmhouse for lunch. Mark's mother and father were there, obviously waiting for me. "We want to show you something," his father said, taking a wallet out of his pocket. "They found this on Mark when he was killed. We thought you might recognise it." Opening the billfold, he carefully removed two worn pieces of notebook paper that had obviously been taped, folded, and refolded many times. I knew without looking that the papers were the ones on which I had listed all the good things each of Mark's classmates had said about him.

"Thank you so much for doing that," Mark's mother said. "As you can see, Mark treasured it." Mark's classmates started to gather around us. Charlie smiled rather sheepishly and said, "I still have my list. It's in the top drawer of my desk at home." Chuck's wife said, "Chuck asked me to put his in our wedding album." "I have mine too," Marilyn said. "It's in my diary." Then Vicki, another classmate, reached into her pocket book, took out her wallet and showed her worn and frazzled list to the group. "I carry this with me at all times," Vicki said without batting an eyelash. "I think we all saved our lists."

To speak from the heart, to say what we mean without sounding mean, is an essential element of having it both ways. A moment's reflection reminds us that attempts to repress feelings building in the heart cause dis-eases ranging from heartaches to broken hearts. Feelings withheld from expression will ooze out in a variety of indirect forms, ranging from humorous Freudian slips of the tongue, to not-so-funny violent verbal or physical explosions. Furthermore, repressed feelings will often be projected upon another person. Indeed, if the siege continues for any period of time, if we regularly squeeze back feelings bubbling in our hearts, we can experience the lethal consequences of these "heart attacks". Rose Franzblau framed the challenge of avoiding repression and projection this way [9]: "Honesty without compassion and understanding is not honesty, but subtle hostility."

In this and the preceding chapter, we have provided examples taken from true stories and fairy tales of *how* using the **ABCs** tool kit can dramatically alter the win-win quality of our relationships. Maintaining a high level of Awareness of our Behaviour and its Consequences is the key to allowing ourselves to hear the voice of our Higher Power, of God, speaking to and through us, while hopefully avoiding the lost opportunities Bambi and his father suffered.

Let us now explore how our ABCs tool kit can help us to deal with a thorny problem: namely, that a rose by any other name may, indeed, not be a rose!

Chapter Five

"What is this thing called love?"

"The great tragedy of life is not that men perish but that they cease to love."

HAVING IT BOTH WAYS is a daunting task. To quote Leo Buscaglia [10], it demands that "you want to give the best *you* there is. And that means developing all the wonder of you ... as a unique human being." He went on to suggest that the *potential returns* for two people being willing to make such an *investment* in one another was the opportunity, "reflecting in each other's love", to "*see infinity*". (Emphasis not in original.)

When two people are in love, they are granted the opportunity to *see infinity*. When a bird appears out of the boundless regions of space and plucks a moth from before our very eyes, or when Sol, the Roman God of the sun, is there when we awaken to life, we feel a similar affinity with infinity. The Infinite Being is often referred to as Godlike, or our Higher Power

Alongside such spiritually heady stuff as the infinity of personal loving relationships, however, it is not by accident that Buscaglia uses words like "potential returns" and "investment". To keep any relationship thriving requires the same kind of attention to detail that characterises any successful business.

Indeed, our relationship jargon is replete with familiar business terminology. Two people often *lose interest* in one another. Their *rate of exchange* plummets. The *debt load* of unexpressed emotional baggage drives the relationship to the brink of emotional *bankruptcy*. Divorce, legal or emotional—a relationship gone *belly up*—is the result.

Unexpressed minor hurts and irritations, like a set of books not shown to the IRS, are often used to justify less than win-win behaviours. A snide remark, a ping, a little dig, seemingly balances the hidden accounts. Who among us has not enjoyed the taste of a silent smirk of self-righteousness? Loneliness is the price exacted from those who must be right all the time.

Letting go of resentments requires both honest feedback—owning and voicing the feeling someone's behaviour caused—and forgiveness—giving up on hopes for the past—so the future can unfold without any *carry forward* losses. Otherwise, ego-driven pride will become the breeding ground of "Eleanor Rigby, Father McKenzie, and all the other lonely people" referred to in the Beatles song.

Having it both ways requires a careful look at how individually we account for the relationship investments we make in one another. To begin to get an appreciation for the depth and breadth of this challenge, we need to find a way to get our hands around a question Cole Porter laid before us [11]:

"What is this thing called love?
 This funny thing called love?
 Just who can solve its mystery?
 And why should it make a fool of me?"

To gain some insight into this mystery, let's look at a familiar, stereo-typical example.

Imagine that your husband has got one of those 'knock-you-out' flus. Everything aches. There is no magical pill he can take to ease the pain. You know your husband would like to feel cared for—to receive comfort, love, and understanding. You would like to comfort him and express your genuine love by caring for him, by giving to him.

In spite of your own busy schedule, you stop by the supermarket to get all the fresh ingredients needed to make a pot of home-made chicken soup—the "good for the soul" kind! Two hours later, you are carrying a steaming hot bowl upstairs. Two minutes later, you are heading back downstairs, steaming over the ungrateful reception you got. A half-hearted grunt of "thank you", from under a squashed pillow and comments such as "It's probably too hot to eat. Besides, I'd rather feed myself. Just leave it and I'll get to it when it cools off" were not particularly good soup for your soul. Having it both ways has turned to both of you feeling rotten!

An unpublished poem [12] portrays this all too painful and familiar scenario between intimate couples.

"Words fill with noise the empty space between,
Wild gesture hides, the message goes unseen,
Uncaring, we cast our thoughts into space,
Unhearing, we heed not nor them embrace.
Paired in a dance, each different music hears,
Confusing the sadness of a smile with joyful tears.
Constrained by fear our ignorance conspires
To keep us from that cup which each desires,
To share the joy of symbiotic living
And reap the gifts born of the gift of giving."

What is happening in the example above that keeps two people "from that cup each desires?" Very simply, you and your husband have natural and normal different definitions of the behaviours each of you need to experience *under these circumstances* for each of you to conclude you are being comforted, understood, and loved.

Most men (recall, that we are talking stereotypically) who are ill feel really cared for when they can be left alone to retire to the safety of their cave and nurse their wounds. They prefer not to have to carry on any conversations with anyone, least of all the person around whom it is most important that they appear strong and all together. Your offer to feed him reminds your husband of how out-of-control and helpless he feels, pouring salt on his already wounded pride.

You, his stereotypical female counterpart, are likely to feel cared for—comforted, loved, and understood—by exactly the opposite behaviours. A bowl of soup would be lovely. Freshly made would be even more sweet and thoughtful. Particularly when accompanied by some tender empathic conversation, the perfect remedy for whatever ails you.

Were the shoes reversed and it were you with the flu—you needing to receive and his needing to give—our stereotypical man would have done his best to be quiet, to stay out of your hair and to let you just rest. In addition to the aches and pains of your flu, you'd also have the feeling of not being cared for, of not being comforted, of being ignored.

In the absence of information to the contrary, you have made an assumption and a normal mistake: you inadvertently enacted an old Biblical rule. *You did unto an other as you would have them do unto you.*

How can we say that living a Biblical truth is a mistake? First, all behaviour, intended or otherwise, has consequences. Second, symbiosis refers to a relationship between two dissimilar organisms. What's similar about human beings is their need for comfort, understanding, and love. What's dissimilar is the specific concrete behaviours each has to experience from the other to feel that needs are being satisfied. Not accounting for these dissimilarities is the breeding ground for relationships that operate in the red.

"Doing unto others as you would have them do unto you" means imposing your definition of goodness on the other person. I comfort you in the ways I need to be comforted. I express understanding in ways that reflect how you would need to behave for me to feel understood. I love you in the ways I would need for you to behave for me to feel loved. When I sense you have a need for love, comfort, or understanding, I choose behaviours I would want to receive if I had similar needs.

While my intention is to be other-directed, notice that the entire focus of my behaviour is self-directed. My uniqueness becomes the template through which I see and experience your uniqueness. What I see when I look at you is a reflection of me. You begin to cease to exist as other than a shadow of me. Your needs are unmet, and I feel resentful at your lack of gratitude for my efforts. Lose-lose relationships lurk in the darkness of these shadows. To paraphrase an old Sufi saying: "Two birds so tied together will not be able to fly, even though they now have four wings".

To move from I and me to we and us requires a reframing of this Biblical truth. If I am in a symbiotic relationship with a significant other that I would like to maintain as win-win, I need to be prepared to "*Do unto the other as <u>they would have me do unto them</u>*".

How do we manifest this reframed Biblical truth? We need to engage in a dialogue the objective of which is an increased understanding *on both our parts* of the specific observable behaviours we each need to experience to feel that our needs are being met by the relationship. We need to reopen our **ABCs** tool kit and *Pull* information about the specific behaviours we need from each other. We each need to Ask questions such as: What am I doing that makes you happy/unhappy, understood/misunderstood, loved/unloved? What can I do differently/more of/less of that will make you more happy, loved, etc.? The attitude we communicate when doing so needs to be one of inquiry versus inquisition.

Our *Push* responses to these *Pull*s need to be stated honestly, reasonably, and with compassion. Blame has no place in a win-win exchange of Appreciates, Prescribes, and Describes. We need to Attend to, Understand, and Empathise with this information as an opportunity for sincere reflection and contemplation without knee-jerk deflection and defensive *Push*ing back.

Doing so will enhance our **ABCs**. Does this **A**wareness guarantee that we will exhibit the **B**ehaviours requested and achieve the Consequences? As a current rent-a-car ad puts it: "Well, not exactly". I may, for example, have a skill deficit. Without the benefit of skill building and practice, I can't deliver what you need. Until I can become versatile through skill practice, we must continue to rely upon our **ABCs** Tool Kit and engage in a dialogue to explore any alternative behaviours I feel able to exhibit now that will still meet your needs.

When sincere efforts are made to deliver on a *Prescribe*—"I need you to stop/start ..."—we need to be patient with and supportive of one another. Learning to exhibit new and different behaviours is a painfully slow process of small steps forward. I may also find I need to request a quid pro quo—something in return—to help me deliver on your need. If your definition of feeling loved requires that I share with you how I'm feeling about myself, I may need for you not to express your judgements about my feelings. In other words, we need to renegotiate our contract—our mutual understanding of how we behave towards one another. Again, we have to be in dialogue.

Last, it is possible that what you are asking of me is understood. I am capable of doing it but doing so would violate a value of mine. If I were to do what you are asking of me to make our relationship better, my relationship with my Inner self, my soul, would suffer. A relationship that results in my feeling that I have to prostitute my self is not, by our definition, a win-win relationship. Someone who, themselves, feels like a loser is a poor partner for any business.

For example, if you kept asking me to tell your mother you were out when she called because you didn't want to talk to her, I might be compromising my sense of honesty. Exchanging our self-respect and dignity to make someone else happy at our expense are devil's bargains. These unhealthy, "If you loved me you'd ...", kind of hostage dynamics many couples get into are not conducive to win-win relationships.

The tension of having to balance a desire to meet our partner's needs and our own conscience cannot be avoided. Love will always win only if we are prepared to give and take to and from one another, equally. It is this equality that ultimately distinguishes the traditional business relationship from the business of living together in an intimate partnership. In business, the main objective is to win by assuming responsibility to negotiate for your own needs. Love is different. In these moments, we are reminded that there resides deep within each of us a higher-order goodness, awaiting the opportunity to speak to us.

This "thing called love" is about investing the energy it takes to ensure that **both** you *and* your partner have an **equal opportunity** at having it both ways.

The "business terms" which guide such win-win relationships represent a psychological, not a legal, contract. You might reflect for a moment upon whether or not you would be prepared to mentally affix your signature to a contract such as the following.

> I will struggle to learn how to identify, voice, and negotiate for the satisfaction of my needs **and** do what I can to help you do the same.
> I accept that I am 100% accountable for my half of our relationship. I will accept any and all the help you can give me in handling that responsibility.

Substituting respect and collaboration among work colleagues as the glue that holds these win-win relationships together does not change this perspective. Respect has the same two dimensions as love: one, avoiding intrusion of my self upon the self of an other, and, two, conscious efforts on my part to increase the esteem with which the other holds him or herself.

The crucial point is that we all agree on certain lists of terms that define a mutually profitable relationship—e.g. open, honest, loving, respectful, trusting, and the like. The problem with these ideal qualities is their abstractness. What they actually mean is subject to interpretation. In any given relationship, the only interpretation that matters is the one made by the parties to the relationship, particularly the receiver of the quality or, if you will, the consumer. We have to move from the abstract—"You don't love me!"—to the concrete—"I need for you to stop criticising me and start praising me. Then I will feel more loved by you".

Used lovingly and with understanding, our **ABCs** tool kit gives us what we need to solve the mystery of what "this thing called love", or comfort, or understanding is all about. Using our Push skills, we can each move from the abstract to the concrete. At the same time, we can each use our Pull skills to help a significant other to make concrete their needs. When two parties to a relationship are using their Push and Pull skills in this way, they can indeed share in the joy of seeing infinity. They can both have it both ways.

To reap these gifts, we must also be cautious not to fall into some very typical and inviting behavioural traps. Moving forward without a conscious awareness of these pitfalls will lead us to other than win-win consequences.

Chapter Six

Pitfalls to be avoided

T HE **ABCs** tool kit must be used skilfully and appropriately to have the win-win effects from which we get these special spiritual feelings. Let us begin by examining a few pitfalls in terms of our use of energy.

Push-Pull energy pitfalls

Assertively using *Push* energy is not the same as being aggressively pushy—raising one's voice, pounding the table, grabbing more than one's share of air time. Nor is it the same as being passively aggressively pushy—stares that could kill, whining rather than reasonably stating one's needs. We are talking about direction of energy flow—from me towards you.

Two people using their energy to *Push* at the same instant are crossing purposes. One person interrupting another in mid-sentence cuts into the other's energy flow. Shouting, yelling, and ominous staring are aggressive ways of using *Push* energy to get someone else to back down. Resentment at not being listened to can lead to shutting the other out. Two people trying to *Pull* one another into the conversation, by asking a question at the same instant also creates static. A kind of "tug-of-war" can result, that reflects the familiar Alphonse-Gaston routine at a doorway. One says "You first" and the other responds "No, be my guest" and neither one moves forward.

By contrast, the energy flow in a win-win relationship functions like the pistons in a car. Both compression, *Push*, and decompression, *Pull*, strokes must be balanced, working to their mutual benefit. If not, several dysfunctional consequences occur. The driver of the car notices a lack of smoothness. The car bucks and stutters. Fuel consumption goes down. Precious fuel energy is wasted. The carburettor can get clogged and full of sludge, further exacerbating these conditions. Periodically, the driver may get the scare of his or her life—the loud explosion of an engine backfiring.

Relationships will also periodically get out-of-sync and may require a tune-up. They lose their spark. Heated blow-ups, when one person has swallowed too much emotional sludge, are not uncommon. Over the long term, any symbiotic relationship will suffer the same consequences as our car's pistons if both parties do not have equal opportunities to *Push* and *Pull*.

Style pitfalls within *Push* energy

Within each of the *Push* and *Pull* energy modes, there are also several pitfalls to be avoided. For example, we noted that Describe and Prescribe form a natural combination. However, one without the other can contribute to relationship tensions. We all know people who pile reason upon reason but never seem to get to the point. They debate and Describe us to death but never seem to Prescribe their solution. An overuse of Describe often leaves these receivers feeling bored by and bored into by the speaker. Vague and ambiguous Prescribes cause static and distortion as well. An ambiguous order, "I need you to pull your weight around here", is quite different from a specific Prescribe "I need you to do the dishes tonight".

Conversely, there are people who seldom ever Describe and explain the basis for their decisions. People act as if they have the divine rights of Kings. They Prescribe "Do this!" without supporting rational Describes other than "Because I said so, that's why!" Haughty people who talk down to others from thrones of self-appointed superiority do not enjoy win-win relationships. Their charges smile lamely and tune them out.

Patterns such as these will reflect themselves in the appearance of inappropriate music and dance. After a machine gun burst of Describes without a Prescribe, voice volume begins to rise as if to say, "Come on, stupid! You're missing my point!" At the same time, the other person is wondering, "Come on! What is your point?" Bodies stiffen. Frustration rises. Fingers start shaking in blame versus pointing to details. This is not fertile ground upon which to grow win-win outcomes. Such static will cause senders and receivers to feel as if they are on different wavelengths, to feel out of touch.

Because they involve feelings directly, Appreciates and Inspires must be approached with equal sensitivity. Loading a person with praise as a prelude to piling on more work will boomerang. While specificity adds value to an Appreciate, dumping a history of stored criticism all at once is not the way to a win-win. Finally, to qualify as a heartfelt Inspire, our encouragement must be unqualified. You might try to Inspire someone by saying: *Your speech will leave them gasping for breath*! However, if you then add the phrase *I think,* you may well douse the very spark of enthusiasm you tried to kindle.

Style pitfalls within *Pull* energy

On the *Pull* side, most of us are quite sensitive to the cues another person is giving off that they are selectively Attending to what we are saying. Saying, *I'm listening,* while continuing to shuffle papers will create a mixed message. We get defensive when Ask behaviours are being misused. Leading the witness by using questions designed to *Pull* a person around to my position (or entrap them) feels like an inquisition—*Why did you mess that up?* They will not be as well received as open-ended inquiries—*Can you describe how that happened?*

Finally, Empathy (often confused with sympathy, a point we will address in a subsequent chapter) may lighten someone's emotional load. However, seeking Empathy by whining is a form of manipulation. Some people incessantly complain *Poor me! Poor me!* This is the mark of a person who is making themselves into a victim. The kind who, when they get a speeding ticket, laments: *If the policeman had been doing his real job, I'd have never been given the speeding ticket.* It is very difficult to manifest Empathy when someone's sharing their feelings is being used as a vehicle to unload responsibility for solving their problems onto your shoulders. Such a pattern will leave you feeling used.

The pitfalls in action

Imagine your teenage child has been getting home for dinner consistently late. As the father, you say: "Your mother and I have discussed your being habitually late for dinner. We suggest you be home tonight by 6:00 p.m. sharp, or we'll have to ground you for the weekend."

As an attempt to influence your daughter's behaviour, there is nothing wrong with this statement. From a style point of view, what you've done is mix a clear *Describe*—"Your mother and I have discussed your being habitually late for dinner"—with, at best, a very weak *Prescribe*—"We suggest you be home tonight by 6:00 p.m. sharp, or we'll have to ground you for the weekend".

What makes the Prescribe weak is the use of *We* versus *I*. If she's inclined to make your lives difficult, your daughter knows exactly how to respond! The next thing you know, you and your spouse are having a heated argument with her about how the two of you are always ganging up on her or how her friends' parents don't make them get home for dinner. If she's really good at it, your daughter will be able to get you two into an argument with each other by using the divide-and-conquer strategy of playing up to one of you at the other's expense: "It isn't my fault, mom, that you couldn't go out for the tennis team when you were in school" or "Dad, you told me I shouldn't be so shy, that I should make an effort to make more friends".

This vignette could be cleaned up style-wise in the following manner: "Your mother and I have discussed your being habitually late for dinner. *(Describe)* If you're not home tonight by 6:00 p.m. sharp, I've decided I'm going to ground you for the weekend. (*Prescribe*.) Your mother is in perfect agreement with this decision." (*Describe*.)

The point is that to say that *We are proposing* ... is perfectly okay but it is not a strong *Prescribe*. Rather, it is a *Describe*, a reporting of a poll taken to prove how many people support a particular idea. The *Push* comes from the weight of the numbers (*We suggest* ...) in contrast to my personal assertion, *I suggest* ...

This I versus We distinction is also at the core of many an Appreciation-lined pitfall. Personal judgements are a fact of life. When I choose to provide <u>direct, face-to-face</u> feedback about how <u>I</u> feel about another person's past or current behaviour or ideas, I am using my *Push* energy to Appreciate.

Why the emphasis on direct, face-to-face and *I*? One, if I tell Mary how I feel about John ("John is the most thorough engineer I know!"), it is not an Appreciate. I am *Describing* to Mary how I feel about a third party. It isn't until I tell John how I feel about him ("You are the most thorough engineer I know.") that it becomes an *Appreciate*. Two, Prescribe and Appreciate get their power from personal ownership through the use of I statements. This is particularly the case in extremely challenging interpersonal situations where the feeling we are struggling to communicate is one of constructive criticism, of dislike or disappointment.

Constructive criticism—the communication of dislikes, of disappointments—requires that we must broaden our understanding of the word Appreciate. Webster's Dictionary tells us that to appreciate is "to raise in value; to exercise wise judgement, delicate perception, and keen insight in realising worth".

Our ability to grow and develop—to fully realise our potential, value and worth—depends upon learning how to be better tomorrow than we are today. When we have people in our lives who are willing and able "to exercise wise judgement, delicate perception, and keen insight" in the feedback they provide, we are helped to further "realise our worth". We become a better partner in our relationship. Fully Appreciating each other's strengths and opportunities for growth is a sure strategy for having it both ways.

Another reason has to do with the fact that enormous amounts of human energy get wasted by what we call the triangle game. Person A talks about Person B, usually in a non-complimentary manner, behind their back to Person C. Such character assassination has no place in our win-win scheme. Whether the Emperor has no clothes on or is clad in the most beautiful suit, he deserves the respect of being spoken to directly.

A final Appreciation pitfall concerns the specificity of our praise and constructive criticism and the power of combining a Describe along with an Appreciate. One without the other can contribute to less-than-optimal relationships. Certainly, it feels good to hear that "Your report was terrific", a general non-specific *Appreciate*. But, it is even better to know specifically, via added *Describes*, what to be sure to repeat: "There were no typos and all of your research was current". This detail helps you enjoy that same good feeling again. Had you been told that the report was less than terrific, you would have felt not so good. Again, a detailed Describe would be invaluable as a means of knowing what to do differently next time so you could both feel better [13].

Avoiding the pitfalls: a sample scenario

Let's take a moment and see how these pieces might fit together in a work-related situation. Hilda has been with the company for 25 years. In reviewing her record when you took over three years ago, you noted that she had started as a filing clerk and worked her way up to her current position as the main receptionist, a position she's held for 10 years. Her efficiency, personal grooming, and consistency (seldom missing even a day's work) were noted by all of her previous supervisors. Born and raised in Germany, she married an American soldier and returned to the United States with him. She seldom appears happy and doesn't socialise with the other employees other than recognising them with a "Good morning!"

You've received periodic complaints in the past from customers that she's been rude to them. When you've talked with her regarding these complaints, she always seemed to have a justifiable answer. But in the past month, there have been three complaints regarding her demeanour.

The letter you've just read is from the wife of a prominent local attorney stating that Hilda's rudeness ended with Hilda shouting a profanity at her.

Something has to be done. In the quiet of your office, you reflect on what might have made your prior feedback ineffective, and on what to say to Hilda now. Your secretary has just buzzed you announcing that Hilda is on her way in.

"Good afternoon, Hilda. Have a seat please."

Hilda sits down, crosses her legs and nervously adjusts her skirt, avoiding any eye contact.

"Hilda, we've talked in the past about the customer complaints I had received regarding your behaviour. Just this month I've received three more, and this month this one from Mrs. Polanski is very ..."

Before you can finish your opening *Describe* remarks, Hilda interrupts: "Well, no one is perfect ... including you and that lady!"

We invite you to take a moment now and reflect on what your own typical reaction as a boss would be to Hilda right now.

Notice whether it is a *Push* or a *Pull* or a combination. Would your response—words, music, and dance—be harsh or compassionate? Would you intend to get even for the accusation that you, too, might be imperfect or attempt to get the conversation back on an even keel? What are your options here?

Obviously, pulling rank would be easy. A silent *Prescribe*, a nonverbal stern look, and a pointed finger would be all the music and dance needed to get Hilda to be quiet, or to up and quit. Depending on the human resource policies and rules in operation, you might even be able to end the conversation right now and put her on immediate probation. In other words, you can have it your way without regard for Hilda.

Because all behaviour has consequences, there would be a price to pay for taking the easy way out. Both you and Hilda know you hold an ace card you can play any time you choose. The real question is, "What are the other alternatives available to you, and what price tags do they carry?" Let's look at a few.

- "I'm sorry, Hilda. *(Appreciate)* I can imagine that my calling you into my office in the middle of the day would make you nervous. *(Empathy)* I need you to hear me out and not be defensive." *(Prescribe)* Or, "Is there anything I can do to help you be less defensive?" *(Ask)*
- "It sounds like Mrs. Polanski did something that you feel justified your behaviour. *(Understand)* Can you tell me your side of what happened?" *(Ask)*

- "Nothing Mrs. Polanski did or said can justify the disrespectful language she says you used. (*Describe*) That can never happen again. (*Prescribe*) Now, tell me what she did that got you so upset." (*Prescribe*)
- "It sounds as if you've got some feedback to give me. (*Understand*) I'll be very happy to hear it after we've resolved this situation." (*Prescribe*)

This list of examples could go on at some length. Like the spices in a well-stocked kitchen, the eight *Push* and *Pull* styles lend themselves to an enormous diversity of combinations and permutations. Your first choice is whether to shoot from the hip or give yourself some time to let your mind reflect on other possibilities that have a chance, at a minimum, of not worsening the situation. The former keeps your ego feeling strong and in control. The latter depends on what in your heart you feel is best.

In your heart, do you truly believe it is worthwhile to strive for commitment versus compliance? Are you willing to work for a possible—albeit not guaranteed—win-win outcome, or are you simply more interested in cutting your losses? Does investing the energy it takes to help another human being grow and develop (versus shooting them down) bring any real return to you? Conversely, do you look at situations where others disappoint you as opportunities for self-improvement, where, by looking in the mirror, you can expand your Awareness of your own Behaviour and its Consequences?

These are not easy questions to address. Nor should they be. Having it both ways is not for the faint-hearted.

In ensuing chapters, we will see more clearly how these *Push* and *Pull* ingredients, and avoiding their pitfalls, can be used to spice up the win-win quality of any relationship.

Chapter Seven

Pregnant moments in intimate relationships

IN OUR RELATIONSHIPS with loved ones, moments periodically occur that are alive with possibilities. We've all been there. The hair on the back of your neck is electric. Palms are sweaty. Stomach knotted. A question mark hangs like a balloon in the air. Your response will either cause the balloon to burst and send your relationship into a tail-spin or send it soaring to a new level of honesty and realness.

As an example, let's use a kitchen scene between a husband and wife, a 60 second slice in time pregnant with a range of possibilities for affecting a relationship for a long time.

One truth or many?

You arrive home from work, bone weary from another Saturday spent fighting off the down-sizing alligators. A hot bath, a pizza, and a video movie would be heavenly. The first thing that catches your eye as you enter the kitchen is a mountain of pots and pans on the counters. Simultaneously, your nostrils sense an unfamiliar aroma and your husband's voice pipes up, "Come and have a taste. My mother said it was a terrific new pot roast. She had it at a friend's luncheon the other day."

You successfully navigate around the drippings on the floor, but the sleeve of your favourite cashmere sweater brushes a dirty utensil. As you swallow the spoonful being held out for you to taste, your taste buds plead "Please do not repeat!"

"So, what do you think?" your husband asks expectantly, stretching tired and pained back muscles. "Come on, be honest, the truth." The truth is you want to bite your tongue and say nothing.

In any human interaction, there are multiple truths. This is, in part, the case because we are all a collage of different—and often conflicting—feelings and thoughts. Our total selves are, therefore, like a prism. Different situations can act to bring to light, to bring centre stage, different combinations of our complex human natures. We still love deeply the child that has screamed half the night, and, yet, another part of us feels like screaming back at the child to "Shut up ... or else!"

Our **ABCs** tool kit offers a variety of ways to proceed to increase the possibility that we can show an aspect of the best sides of ourselves that lies within each of us, and not succumb to the shadow sides that also reside in each of us. In exploring the alternatives available, the two questions Neale Donald Walsch offered as the keys to developing a "Friendship With God" [14] can be extremely useful: (1) Is this who I am? and (2) What would love do now?

Question (1) drives us to find a way to speak the truth in our hearts. Anything less than that truth means that the answer to "Is this who I am?" is "I am a dishonest person". Treating our souls, the place where the best of us resides, to regular doses of lies will erode any chance of a win-win relationship because we are treating our Inner Selves as losers.

Question (2) motivates us to behave as the honest person who represents "Who I am" in a way (with words, music and dance) that fits our heartfelt understanding of "What love would do now?" Will my actions be based on understanding and loving kindness?

In other words, **the effort to be honest with ourselves must be matched by an <u>equal effort</u> to be compassionate with the other person**.

Any time we select a behaviour to exhibit towards ourselves and/or someone else that meets these two criteria—reflecting who I am (honesty with ourselves) AND what love (compassion with the other person) would do now—God, our Higher Power is, by definition, speaking to and through us.

Your husband's question, "What do you think?" leaves you poised on the razor's edge of a challenge Rose Franzblau defined for us earlier: "Honesty without compassion and understanding is not honesty, but subtle hostility".

Some partial responses

Each of several *partial* responses will reflect one truth in this pregnant moment.

- "I can imagine this was not an easy recipe to prepare with everything else you had to do today." (*Empathise*)
- "Can you imagine how the subtle taste of the saffron could be enhanced next time by using less of the chilli peppers!" (*Inspire*)

- "You couldn't have known that I had Mexican food for lunch, and it left a strong taste in my mouth. I'm not sure all of the spices you used got through to my taste buds." *(Describe)*
- "I'm wiped out and I'm not sure I can give a meal like this a fair test tonight. *(Describe)* How about we hold it until tomorrow and I'll try it again." *(Prescribe)*
- "I can see how hard you've worked on this surprise. *(Empathise)* I thank you for being so willing to experiment. *(Appreciate)* Your mother and I have always had different tastes." *(Describe)*
- "I wish I could say I loved it. *(Describe)* But it isn't my cup of tea. *(Appreciate)* Have you thought of inviting your parents to come and share it?" *(Ask)*

These responses are not merely polite ways of avoiding the truth. They are labelled *partial* to emphasise the point that, while your first reaction is to phone for a pizza, all of the other statements could also be reflective of truths in this situation. Let us examine how our two criteria might impact these examples.

Knowing what you know about yourself—what you ate for lunch, how you react to being bone weary after having to work another weekend, your reactions to seeing a mountain of pots and pans needing to be cleaned when all you were dreaming about was a hot tub and a pizza— ask yourself: "Is it possible that you might have a different reaction if you were to taste it again tomorrow?" If your honest answer to that question is "No way! Never!" you cannot, for example, truthfully *Prescribe*—"How about we hold it until tomorrow and I'll try it again."

To continue our example, <u>if</u> you are an accomplished cook and your palate can distinguish the subtle taste of saffron and how it can be muted by too many chilli peppers, you can, with integrity, *Inspire* your husband to try the recipe again. This same truth from your personal experience and culinary skill is what allows you to be truthful when you compassionately *Describe*, as a part of your response, that you had Mexican food for lunch.

The bottom line *Appreciate* statement with respect to the special meal that your husband cooked remains: "It's not a taste I enjoy. Thank you for making it."

Your husband might have several reactions. At the positive extreme, perhaps with a tinge of disappointment in his voice, he might say: "I guess I should have called and asked you if you felt like meat, but I wanted to surprise you." The following reaction from the wife would not jar our senses: "And a pleasant surprise it is. You're so thoughtful."

On the other hand, we would be jolted if the husband's reaction was: "What do you mean! Damn it!! I can't ever seem to please you, can I!" If they've been enjoying a win-win symbiotic relationship and the husband's remark was totally out of character, the intensity of his angry aspersion will catch the wife off-guard. A rising of tension in her neck muscles, a furrowed brow, or an angry barb rising to the tip of her tongue would be normal initial reactions. Hopefully, her reaction will not be an equal unkindness: "Well that's a fine 'How do you do!' you@*#!"

A middle-of-the-road response from the husband might be "What a waste! I should have taken a nap instead!" followed by a nonverbal throwing down of his apron. Again, if they've enjoyed a mutually positive relationship, the wife is likely to exhibit a non-defensive and puzzled series of *Pulls*: "Wow! Where did that come from? (*Ask*) You sound really upset about something. (*Empathise*) What's going on? (*Ask*)" This act of non-blaming inquiry versus accusatory inquisition on her part provides him the opportunity to reflect on the consequences of his behaviour. An ensuing *Appreciate* apology and possible *Descriptive* explanation opens the door for a productive conversation: "I'm sorry, hon. I'm really teed off at my boss. I worked all week on a damn report for him and all he can say is: 'Good training for my job.' I didn't mean to take it out on you."

So, while both of them will not be eating pot roast for dinner this evening, the skilful use of the **ABCs** tool kit can help to ensure that their relationship that evening did not also turn sour. The key questions to consider are: "What are truths for you in a given ticklish situation?" and "Are you willing to invest the 'split second' it takes to look into your heart and ask yourself 'What would love do now?'"

The recipe your spouse made had many different spices. The truth is also made up of multiple ingredients. Identifying them and thinking about how to put them together can dramatically influence the taste your response leaves in your spouse's mouth. At least, thinking through your options will minimise the possibility of including in your response to your spouse's "Come on, be honest, the truth!" the two things you are most likely to regret: "There goes your mother again, trying to poison me!" and "I love it, I really love it!" The former could unleash a stream of reactions not likely to be win-win, but very likely to make the downsizing alligators look like pussycats! The latter can have long-term negative consequences, as the following true story will attest.

During the early 1940s, my first wife's mother and new stepfather were invited to an aunt's house for Thanksgiving dinner so the family could get to know the new groom. In honour of the occasion, a special old family version of plum pudding was prepared. It was a painstaking process using only the finest ingredients and the oldest of brandies.

At dessert time, with great fanfare, the flaming pièce de résistance was placed in front of the guest of honour. In spite of urging to "Eat! Eat!", he served himself a tiny portion. He then patted his overly stuffed belly, nonverbally justifying his constraint. He tasted the pudding and praised it to the roof. A similar set of *Describes*—"I've had double portions of everything today"—were offered a few moments later as excuses so he could gracefully excuse himself. He simply could not fit another spoonful into his stomach. He then repeated his *Appreciate* for the umpteenth time: "But, I absolutely love the pudding!"

Until his death several decades later, Thanksgiving with the family had a very familiar soap opera quality. The aunt would phone weeks before the event to assure him that she'd be making his favourite dessert again. And, as if he could forget, she'd remind him that she didn't go through this painful, time-consuming ritual for just anybody! Indeed, she had taken to making two of them so he could have one to take home and enjoy throughout the holidays.

The ride to the aunt's house should have been filled with good cheer. Instead, it was consumed with angst. The icy silence in the front seat was melted periodically with heated comments about the various prices each parent felt they had to pay for being connected to the other's family. The children huddled in the back seat had to be extra good and not do anything to upset their father. They were to keep quiet and never repeat anything that they heard their parents discussing, least of all that their father abhorred plum pudding!

This soap opera is familiar to all of us. What varies are the details of the particular scripts we have trained ourselves to deliver. As André Berthiaume [15] put it, "We all wear masks, and the time comes when we cannot remove them without removing some of our own skin."

Bending the truth is not the same as repackaging multiple truths in a way that makes them more palatable. The wife whose husband made a special meal could have, herself, arrived home in a tense, angry, mood after another day fighting off the down-sizing alligators. Without thinking, she could have taken her frustration out on her husband. In other words, both of them—both parties to any relationship —have an equal opportunity to make it turn sour, or keep it spicy and alive. Careful packaging will increase the likelihood that our spoonfuls of honesty— essential to striving to be who we are—are spiced with equal doses of compassion and understanding—essential to striving to do what love would do now—and not overly laced with traces of subtle hostility.

Chapter Eight

The gift is in the giving

HAVING IT BOTH WAYS with win-win relationships is an ideal our hearts embrace. Real life doesn't always work that way. No matter how hard the couple in the prior kitchen example tried, their efforts to do the right thing might have fallen short of their spiritual ideal.

Relationships go through ups and downs. Some swings are of short duration while others persist. When a downswing continues to spiral like a plane in a steep nose-dive, bailing out seems easier than trying to pull up. Husbands and wives go through bitterly contested divorces. Intimate pillow talk is replaced by icy silence. Parents and children become estranged, finding bonds of flesh and blood insufficient to bridge differences in values. Friends have falling-outs that never get repaired.

No matter how hard we strive to maintain an Awareness of our Behaviour and its Consequences in our communications, relationships bleed, become ill ... and sometimes die. No matter how hard two people might try, a win-win outcome may not result. This painful reminder that progress, not perfection, is our lot in life raises an importance issue. If win-lose is a mythical outcome, when a relationship fails, temporarily or permanently, does having it both ways have to translate into both of us feeling like losers?

We think not. An old adage reminds us that, "'tis better to have loved and lost than never to have loved at all". Similarly, we believe that sincere and honest efforts aimed at trying to develop and maintain win-win relationships will yield inherent and permanent gifts to the soul. These are gifts we personally might never get to taste were it not for our continuing efforts—trying as they may be—at having it both ways. They transcend the fact that the relationship has died.

Consider how we might respond to the pain of someone who has suffered a death in the family. Helpless to do anything about the person's loss, we strive to do what we can to help heal their wounds. So great is the grief and self-pity that nothing we do or say seems to offer any real solace. No matter how hard we try, the person is not likely to feel better for a long time. What possible gift might ensue from efforts that fail to provide comfort, understanding, and love to someone in dire need?

Empathy versus sympathy

One answer lies in the different roles that sympathy and empathy play in the healing process. Many of us will instinctively rush out to get a sympathy card. A thoughtful gesture, but not to be confused with empathy.

Empathy, from the Greek for affection or passion, is "the projection of one's own personality into the personality of another in order to understand him better". Sympathy, on the other hand, is "sameness of feeling ... especially, pity for another's trouble, suffering, etc.". How do these two qualities differ? And what difference does it make?

Sympathy is *Push*

Sympathetic statements such as "I feel so badly for you" or "I'm so sorry for your loss" reflect *Push* energy intended to console and comfort you. Note that they are I-oriented *Describes*. There may be a "sameness" to the pity or sorrow I feel in response to your suffering, but what I am most in touch with is my feeling, not yours.

Directly on the heels of such sympathetic statements, we often hear things such as: "It reminds me of when my dear ... died. It took a while, but I finally got over it." The underlying message is two-fold. One, there is an implicit *Push Prescribe* embedded in such a reflection. "Don't worry. You'll get over the pain soon". Two, there is often an unspoken projection of personal discomfort hidden behind such sympathy statements: "Your situation has caused me to recall a suffering I might not have otherwise remembered at the moment". Therefore, a subtle pressure is put on the person currently suffering to respond to this *Push*. The person may feel a need to soothe the sympathiser regarding their prior loss. The person's burden may be increased rather than lightened.

Gretel Eherlich [16] reminds us that sympathy in contrast to empathy "may console but [also] often conceals". Heartfelt sympathy may hide similar unresolved pains and hurts not yet healed in the heart of the sympathiser. Recognising this fact within myself—"I am feeling sympathetic"— can increase my own awareness. Increased awareness allows me to take responsibility and accountability for healing some of these wounds I still carry. I am able to look inside myself and ask:

"I wonder what I am trying to tell myself? What can I learn from this? Have I finished grieving the death of 'my dear ...?'"

Empathy is *Pull*

By contrast, empathy reflects *Pull* energy. It positions me alongside you. I strive to dig deeply into my personality, to tap into my existing reservoir of affection or passion. My objective, however, in doing so is to better resonate with what it is that you may be feeling. When I communicate that understanding, you have the chance to feel less alone. Your burden may feel lightened.

When I empathise, I am using my *Pull* energy to enable you to be fully who you need to be at the moment. I don't feel something *for you*—the same thing I'd feel for me. I feel something *with you*. The mirror of *Empathy* is focused on you, not I, not me: "*You* loved each other so deeply. *You* must be feeling devastated/abandoned/crushed".

However, in our efforts to empathise we need to be careful not to express well-intentioned over-statements: "I know just what you're feeling". True empathy occurs when your feeling resonates with one of mine. I can also empathise when I imagine what you might be feeling: "If I were in your shoes, I can imagine I might be feeling really ...". This is not the same as sympathising, as reflecting a "sameness of feeling". I am not walking in my shoes and telling you how I feel—a simpatico. I am trying to project myself into your shoes: "If I were ...". You decide whether or not what I imagine, or what feeling is resonating in me from you in response to you, is how you do feel.

True empathy causes our two separate hearts to resonate in rhythmic unison. By putting myself into your shoes for a moment in time, we both get to experience the gift of oneness. By being willing to resonate with how you are experiencing an important event in your life, I get to feel how I might feel if, or when, I have to walk in similar shoes. By relating to how you must be feeling, I get a taste of how I might be feeling, or a reminder of how I did feel, under similar circumstances. Empathy is a way to having it both ways while sympathy is more limited.

For example, I felt sadness at my father's passing, as I would for any living being, but the tears I shed were of regret for the father I never had, not of deep sorrow for the father I lost. I did not feel the kind of emotional loss someone else would experience whose relationship to their father had been deeply loving and kind. When he died, sympathy from others who had lost a parent, however well-intentioned, left me feeling very misunderstood and unconsoled.

Push Prescribes ("You'll get over it soon". "Keep busy".) got perfunctory head nods from me, but fell on deaf ears. *Pull Asks* ("How are you feeling?") were helpful to a point. I needed to be ready to talk. Empathy was a better medicine for me, especially from those who knew enough about my family history to imagine how I might be feeling at his passing. A dear aunt *Empathise*d: "Knowing some of the problems you had with your father, I can imagine you're feeling a combination of relief and sadness right now". Her response struck a more resonant chord in my heart than any expression of sympathy. As with any well-timed use of *Pull* energy, I felt invited to *Push* out some of the ambivalent feelings lodged in my heart. Being able to do so, to get those feelings off my chest, contributed to my healing.

Empathy manifested in this manner is a powerful example of having it both ways. If I have been able to truly tune in, to get on your wavelength, your feelings become clearer to you. In the non-judgmental safety created by using *Pull* energy, you feel less wary and are willing to express and expand upon those feelings. You glow with the warmth of having been touched.

Your appreciation of my support lifts my spirits. The reservoir of meaningful life experiences stored in my soul has increased. I feel better about myself. I glow with the warmth of having touched and been touched.

A further distinction between empathy and sympathy is important. Sympathy is always focused on suffering, sorrow, pain, and loss. Empathy is not so limited. If I choose to, I can focus the mirror of my *Pull* muscles on your joy and enthusiasm. Rather than trying to *Push* you to greater heights using my own Appreciates and Inspires, I can *Empathise*: "You must be feeling like the 'cat who ate the canary' after having to wait so long to find a publisher for your book!" You are then free to fan your own flames of affection and passion: "You bet I do! I can't wait to start the book signing tour!" By attending carefully to what you say, my own reservoir of affection and passion is increased in scope and breadth. My ability to empathise goes up—a win for me. A potential future win for you, and others.

We are not suggesting that either empathy or sympathy is better. Both sympathy and empathy are instruments that can contribute to our having it both ways. Understanding their uniqueness enhances this potential. A lack of awareness of the "I-oriented" versus "you-oriented" distinction can reduce our ability to consciously choose behaviours more likely to have a certain consequence. The *Pull* of sincere Empathy is more likely to enable another person to open and pour out their hearts than the *Push* of a Described sympathy.

In both cases, I am challenged to dig deeply into myself and ask: "Whose needs am I striving to meet at this moment?" "What are my true motives?" I become a more whole person as a result. The self-insight such reflection affords can only operate to our mutual benefits.

Forgiving and remembering

Fortunately, literal deaths are not the only situations capable of teaching us lessons for living. The death of a relationship—a divorce, the ending of a long-standing partnership or friendship—offers comparable opportunities for having it both ways. Depending upon how we choose to handle these emotional challenges, we can learn much about humility, wisdom, and forgiveness. Consider the following story.

> A young man went to a guru and asked him how he might obtain wisdom. After some thought, the guru responded, "To gain wisdom, my son, you must have good judgement." This response left the young student something to ponder but he wasn't fully satisfied. A few days later, he returned to the master and inquired what it would take to attain good judgement, if that was indeed the path to wisdom. Once again, the guru pondered the question, then smiled saying, "To develop good judgement, you must have a great deal of experience." For a while this answer mollified the young man's curiosity, but seeds of discontent began to blossom. If he needed experience to gain good judgement, and good judgement to gain wisdom, he was led to wonder how he could get the appropriate experience. He once again posed his question to the teacher. Without hesitation, the wise man responded "Oh, that is simple. To get experience, you must exercise a great deal of bad judgement."

As soon as Adam and Eve partook of the tree of knowledge, progress, not perfection became our lot in life. We are, and will remain, imperfect human beings struggling the best we can to do the best we can. As we travel the road to wisdom, we will periodically "exercise bad judgement". We will exhibit behaviours that cause others, and ourselves, pain. Hopefully, we can take actions not to repeat our mistakes, but we cannot expect to prevent them from ever happening.

Imagine that someone you love has done something that has caused you emotional pain. Something greater than a minor irritation—forgetting to meet you for lunch. Less than what we would call a point of no return event—the breaking of a marriage vow. Common folklore would have us strive to "forgive and forget". We believe that the greater challenge, the one that will afford the two parties involved the opportunity for having it both ways, is for *both* to struggle to "forgive and remember".

Both has been emphasised to remind us of the 100%-50% rule. We are each 100% accountable for our half of every relationship. When the fingers of self-righteous blame are pointed at an accused, at least half of those fingers are pointing back at the accuser. While the emotionality will be easier to manage in mistake situations less than spouse infidelity, the challenge of mutual accountability remains. Seldom is an abandoned spouse free of any accountability for a marriage gone sour.

Learning from mistakes, and particularly from painful relationship deaths, will not be helped by a focus on "Who did what?" Consequently, our focus will be: "What can both parties do to try and ensure that they both come away from the mistake feeling comforted, understood, and loved?" "What are the gifts to be gleaned from this struggle?" Because releasing the need to resent, to punish, to get even plays a vital role in having it both ways, let's begin with the forgiving portion.

Forgiveness and apologies: the breeding ground of empathy

A sincere apology, followed by a request for forgiveness, frequently leads to empathy in return. As we formulate such an apology, we can sense a bit of an internal battle raging. On one side, there is the clear awareness that our behaviour has caused someone else pain. We feel badly for having done so. On the other side, our egos are screaming out a host of "Yeah, but!" messages "Yeah, but if he hadn't … I wouldn't have …".

Biting our tongues is painful. We get a glimpse of how hard it actually is to swallow our pride. The reward is a greater reservoir of humility from which to draw deeper empathy in the future. When someone else digs at us, we can recall how hard it was not to do the same ourselves.

The receiver of such an apology will be challenged. Can they, with equal humility and an open mind, explore and own up to their part of the problem? Given our 100%-50% rule, both parties have some accountability for the mistake that took place between them. Both will have apologies to make. Blame and self-righteous anger are a smoke screen clouding mutual learning. They feed lose-lose outcomes, not the win-wins we are seeking.

Can receivers offer an equally sincere and heartfelt apology? Can they accept our apology with grace, with a simple *Appreciate*, a heartfelt and sincere "Thank you?" Many of us deflect an apology: "Oh, don't worry about it. It wasn't such a big deal". Worse, some use the inherent vulnerability in an apology as an opportunity to take advantage, to dig: "If you had listened to me in the first place ...". "One of these days you'll learn to ...". By resisting these perfectly normal human foibles, receivers can also increase their own reservoirs of affection, humility, and the ability to empathise.

By apologising to you and asking—not begging—your forgiveness, I learn how to better apologise to and forgive myself. Forgiving my father for his frequent use of a cat-o-nine tails was a supreme challenge. Until I could forgive myself for the ways I caused my own children pain (fortunately, nowhere near as abusive), it was impossible. Forgiving and accepting myself for my fallible imperfect humanness is a precondition to my ability to forgiving and accepting you for yours. Forgiving myself for the pain I have inflicted on others demands courage, because the effort brings me face-to-face with the meaning of shame. Confronting that quality in myself increases my ability to empathise when someone else feels ashamed.

I sincerely hope that my heartfelt apology will help to soothe the pains and hurts my behaviour (intentional or otherwise) has caused you. Offering an apology is a gift of Appreciation to myself. Accepting the apology is a gift of Appreciation for you.

However, I am not accountable for your decision to accept my apology. Offering the apology is the only way I know to heal the pain I have in my heart for having caused you harm. Healing this pain, these feelings I have about myself, is my accountability. Dealing with any resentment is your accountability. A failure to do so leaves both of us vulnerable to projecting this pain unto others. Let us look briefly at how this process works.

My self-image, like my shadow, goes with me wherever I travel. The constant in all of my relationships is my self and the esteem in which I hold it. Dignity and self-respect are synonymous and infectious, as are ignominy and shame.

Picture, for a moment, how you'd look and feel after you and your spouse had just worked through a tough emotional pinch point. Forgiveness and apologies were mutual and sincere. You'd been graced with the joy of tasting a true win-win relationship. Now imagine that one of your children has just come home from school very upset. The child's self-esteem has been badly bruised by a friend calling them stupid or four-eyes. The enhanced feeling about yourself that you'll be bringing to that relationship can do nothing to hurt your chances of bringing comfort, understanding, and love to a fragile growing self-image.

By contrast, try to imagine how you'd look and feel to this same child if you and your spouse had just tasted the bitter bile that goes along with a lose-lose relationship. What if you continued to beat up on yourself for your part? Human nature being what it is, we are hard-pressed not to share our wealth, and our pain. How we feel about ourselves— good and bad—is infectious.

If these vital lessons are to be of enduring value, I most certainly want to forgive and remember. Continuing recovery as a drug addict and alcoholic is contingent upon this principle. A fearless and thorough moral inventory forces people in recovery to strip away the false comfort of denial. Remembering all of the pain and suffering they've caused themselves and others is essential. Armed with that awareness, they are then called upon to accept accountability for their behaviour and its consequences. They are required to make amends directly to those they have hurt. Attendance at recovery meetings keeps fresh the memory of the pain and suffering their actions caused loved ones and themselves. It not only deters them from beating up on themselves for past mistakes, but also helps them to not be so foolish as to repeat them.

A couple who find that they cannot forgive transgressions enough to keep the marriage together are faced with a similar challenge of recovery. Life must go on. The scars of past damage cannot be wiped away. Can the process of separation be conducted in a way that allows both to walk away feeling as if they have been able to maintain a win-win relationship? If they rely exclusively upon their respective adversarial third parties for communications during the divorce, they may find it equally hard to speak to one another after their divorce. Unresolved internal dialogues can influence how they relate to potentially new significant others. Even if they cannot forgive the other, an other they are never likely to forget, both parties have to forgive themselves. Failure to do so makes it likely that a remarriage will end up looking like a rerun.

Mistakes knowingly repeated time and again are no longer mistakes. They are signs of insane thinking, of not caring about oneself or others. Even the resentments I might have felt at your past actions are invaluable for me to remember. Again, not as a way to justify pain I might have just caused you: "Yeah, well remember when you did ...!" But rather, to help me choose not to cause you and others similar pain and resentments.

Embracing the opportunity to forgive and remember our own and others' mistakes allows healing to replace *heeling*—the shame of having made them. Confidence and gratitude grow to replace arrogance and superiority. Humility replaces humiliation as we both learn we can be humble, and accept our humanness, versus feeling we have to beg forgiveness for being human. Without humility, there would be less motivation to sustain an attitude of striving to having it both ways.

We can only truly live and learn if we have the tools we need to deal with our humanness in humane ways. The **ABCs** tool kit, used with honesty and compassion, will help us to extract life-enhancing gifts such as humility, grace, and forgiveness. Holding back in a relationship for fear of making a mistake leaves our souls feeling incomplete.

The gift is truly in the giving.

Chapter Nine

Hello, goodbye

T HE "WRESTLING MATCH" of our lives, Morrie Schwartz noted, is
spent "somewhere in the middle of [a] series of pulls back and
forth ... where you want to do one thing, but you are bound to
do another ... where something hurts you, yet you know it shouldn't ...
where you take certain things for granted, even when you know you
should never take anything for granted." As a consequence, every middle has both a beginning and an ending. These points are poignantly
captured in several lines of an old Beatles song [©1966 Northern
Songs]:

"You say yes, I say no.
 You say stop and I say go go go (till it's time to go)
 Oh no
 You say goodbye and I say hello.
 I don't know why you say goodbye, I say hello.
 You say why and I say I don't know."

Our focus in this chapter will be upon how the tools in our **ABCs**
tool kit can help us through two particularly pregnant moments in relationships. Can we *Push* and *Pull* ourselves through the awkwardness,
anxiety ("Oh no"), ambivalence ("You say stop and I say go go go ...
till it's time to go") and excitement we often feel at saying hello? Will
these same tools be of value in those painful moments of helplessness
when a long-standing relationship is about to end ("I don' t know why
you say good bye, I say hello")? Will the proper use of our **ABCs** ensure
in both our beginnings and endings, "that Love wins. Love always
wins?"

Let us begin this exploration with a case example, a true story experienced by Tom Campbell. Again, where appropriate, specific *Push* and
Pull styles will be noted.

Breaking the ice

One of the things I do on a regular basis during the six months a year I spend in San Diego is take an early morning walk on the beach. The cool moist morning sea air energises me for the day. While we were preparing this book, I also used that time to mull over ideas.

I noticed another elderly guy walking the beach at the same time every morning. Cane in hand. Trudging along. Eyes peering out from under a Viking's football cap, focused on the ground in front of his feet. On cold mornings, a Viking's jacket complemented the cap. No eye contact with me. Seldom talking to anyone.

Seeing him most mornings, I got to thinking about how lonesome he must be and how he might enjoy having someone to talk with. I tried to visualise the opening scenario. He's sitting on one of the beach walk benches, and I voice an opening Ask to Pull him into a conversation: "Good morning. How about those Vikings?"

The next morning, I saw him seated on the bench. With the appropriate music (a very friendly tone of voice) and dance (a genuine smile), I initiated my plan. "Good morning. How about those Vikings?"

His loud and angry "You're no Viking fan! Get away from me!" left me shocked and I quickly walked away. So much for planning!

My intended consequence—to have a conversation with a stranger and possibly cheer him up—and my actual impact—his belligerent angry shouting response—were miles apart. It led me, initially, to make a host of less than complimentary assumptions about him and why he would bite at my friendly hand. Avoiding any further contact with a silent self-righteous "Miserable old coot, deserves to be left alone", would have been easy to justify. Particularly since we were in the midst of writing the book, I, instead, took it as a challenge.

First, I re-thought my objective and set a more modest one: to get to know his first name. Then I thought about my strategy. How could I get through to this man who now seemed very angry with me? What can I do to get a friendly response? What behaviours could I use?

I found myself rehearsing an Appreciate apology (I'm sorry) and then Attending very carefully. I tried to visualise his possible reactions. If his response was "I don' t know what you're talking about", I imagined I could follow with a Describe: "The other day I tried to start a conversation with you and you seemed to get angry".

The next morning, I caught up to him shuffling along the beach, head down, familiar frown on his face. A deep breath and I said "Good morning".

He looked sideways at me, head barely turning and still bent towards the ground. Catching his eye for a split second under the visor of his Viking's cap, I said, "I apologise".

He didn't say anything but looked dumbfounded and put his palms up, as if to say, "What's going on?" But he remained silent.

I continued to walk alongside of him, and with great effort, remained silently Attending. After a few minutes of awkward silence, I felt forced to offer a gentle Describe: "I think I may have said something to you yesterday that made you angry."

He remained silent for a few seconds and then said "I've been having trouble with my diabetes."

Given several medical challenges of my own, my response, "Sorry to hear that", carried sincere Empathy, as were the Describe and Ask which followed: "I see you walking along every morning and I just wanted to say hello. What's your name?"

"Donald," he mumbled softly, "but you can call me Ski."

"My name's Tom" I said.

With a louder, more lively voice, Donald asked "Where're you from, Tom?"

"I'm from Montana," I replied.

"With a glint in his eye and a smile on his face, he pointed to his cap, "I'm from Minnesota."

The ice had been broken.

We can only speculate on what it was that kept Donald from bolting the second morning when Tom approached him. Like a frightened animal, he could have given off any number of signals to Tom that said "Stay away. Don't you try to get near me again". We choose to believe the old proverb quoted earlier: "What comes from the heart reaches the heart." Donald sensed that Tom had gone into his own heart and searched for a better way to "say hello", one that wouldn't trigger Donald to immediately "say goodbye".

In that soul-searching process, Tom embraced several significant win-win principles. While his intention had been to come across a certain way—in this case as friendly and caring—the actual consequence of his behaviour was to make Donald cross. As fallible imperfect human beings, we all regularly experience gaps between our intentions and the consequences. How we would like to or think we are coming across does not match how we are coming across.

Rather than dwelling on all of the things that might have been wrong with Donald that led to his belligerent response, Tom focused on his own accountability and on his own behavioural choices. He accepted the fact that we are all 100% accountable for our 50% of every relationship. Tom's *Appreciate*—the apology for the unintended consequences of his behaviour—was a powerful *Push*. Humility residing in our hearts can provide the human warmth needed to break many an ice jam in a relationship, be it one just beginning or one that has become frozen over time with coldness.

Sometimes, as our next true story points out, all that is needed to have it both ways is that we be willing to stop interacting with people as if our meter was running.

Slow down please, it's time!

Twenty years ago, I drove a cab for a living. It was a cowboy's life for some-one who wanted no boss. What I didn't realise was that it was also a min-istry. Because I drove the night shift, my cab became a moving confessional. Passengers climbed in, sat behind me in total anonymity and told me about their lives. I encountered people whose lives amazed me, ennobled me, made me laugh and weep. But none touched me more than a woman I picked up late one August night.

I was responding to a call from a small semi-detached house in a quiet part of town. I assumed I was being sent to pick up some party goers, or some-one who had just had a fight with a lover, or a worker going to an early shift at some factory in the industrial part of town.

When I arrived at 2:30 a.m., the building was dark except for a single light in a ground floor window. Under such circumstances, many drivers would just honk once or twice, wait a minute, then drive away. But I had seen too many impoverished people who depended on taxis as their only means of transportation. Unless a situation smelled of danger, I always went to the door. This passenger might be someone who needs my assistance, I reasoned to myself. So I walked to the door and knocked.

"Just a minute," answered a frail, elderly voice. I could hear something being dragged across the floor. After a long pause, the door opened. A small woman in her 80s stood before me. She was wearing a print dress and a pill-box hat with a veil pinned on it, like somebody out of a 1940s film. By her side was a small nylon suitcase. The apartment looked as if no one had lived in it for years. All the furniture was covered with sheets. There were no clocks on the walls, no knickknacks or utensils on the counters. In the cor-ner was a cardboard box filled with photos and glassware.

"Would you carry my bag out to the car?" she asked. I took the suitcase to the cab, then returned to assist the woman. She took my arm and we walked slowly towards the kerb. She kept thanking me for my kindness. "It's nothing," I told her. "I just try to treat my passengers the way I would want my mother treated."

"Oh, you're such a good boy," she said.

When we got in the cab, she gave me an address, then asked, "Can you drive through downtown?"

"It's not the shortest way," I answered quickly.

"Oh, I don't mind," she said. "I'm on my way to a hospice."

I looked in the rear view mirror. Her eyes were glistening. "I don't have any family left," she continued. "The doctor says I don't have very long."

I quietly reached over and shut off the meter. "What route would you like to take?" I asked.

Let us stop for a moment's reflection. Because there is no next day or morning after accountability involved, people will often share their deepest feelings, fears, hopes and concerns with cab drivers, barbers and bar tenders. Yet, we can see that even these fleeting relationships con-tain the seeds of opportunity for something special to occur.

The cab driver had a built-up reservoir of Empathy in his heart—"I had seen too many impoverished people who depended on taxis as their only means of transportation." This gift gave him the courage to do what his colleagues could justifiably *not* do under similar circumstances. "Unless a situation smelled of danger ... I walked to the door and knocked."

When the woman heaped him with *Appreciates*—"She kept thanking me for my kindness", his first reactions were *Describe* deflections: "It's nothing." "I just try to treat my passengers the way I want my mother treated." Not to be dissuaded, the woman delivered an even stronger *Appreciate*: "Oh, you're such a good boy."

In *Describing* "... it's not the shortest way", the cab driver reflected his integrity. He was not a person who sought to win at another's expense. As we shall see as our story concludes, nonverbally shutting off the meter—an act of true compassion—yields the win-win reward we get when we combine integrity with Empathy. These are among the key ingredients needed to allow God to speak to us both.

> For the next two hours, we drove through the city. She showed me the building where she'd once worked as an elevator operator. We drove through the neighbourhood where she and her husband had lived when they were newlyweds. She had me pull up in front of a furniture warehouse that had once been a ballroom where she had gone dancing as a girl. Sometimes she'd ask me to slow in front of a particular building or corner and would sit staring into the darkness, saying nothing.
>
> As the first hint of sun was creasing the horizon, she suddenly said, "I'm tired, let's go now."
>
> We drove in silence to the address she had given me. It was a low building, like a small convalescent home, with a driveway that passed under a portico. Two orderlies came out to the cab as soon as we pulled up. They were solicitous and intent, watching her every move. They must have been expecting her. I opened the trunk and took the small suitcase to the door. The woman was already seated in a wheelchair.
>
> "How much do I owe you?" she asked, reaching into her purse.
>
> "Nothing," I said.
>
> "You have to make a living," she answered.
>
> "There are other passengers," I responded. Almost without thinking, I bent and gave her a hug.
>
> She held onto me tightly. "You gave an old woman a little moment of joy," she said. "Thank you."
>
> I squeezed her hand, then walked into the dim morning light. Behind me, a door shut. It was the sound of the closing of a life.
>
> I didn't pick up any more passengers that shift. I drove aimlessly, lost in thought. For the rest of that day, I could hardly talk. What if that woman had got an angry driver, or one that was impatient to end his shift? What if

I had refused to take the run, or had honked once, and driven away? On a quick review, I don't think I have done anything more important in my life.

We're conditioned to think our lives revolve around great moments. But great moments often catch us unaware—beautifully wrapped in what others may consider a small one.

How often do we allow fleeting hard currencies of metered exchanges—"I'll do XXX for you, but only if you'll do YYY for me"— to take priority over the softer more permanent expressions of unconditional *Appreciation* and *Empathy*? How much time on the meter we allow to run our lives is it worth giving up to hear a dying woman thank you for the gift you've given her of a "moment of joy?" Or to hear a four-year-old child ask if their nose will get bigger if they tell a fib?

The impending *sound of the closing of our own or other's lives* confronts us with our own "what ifs". What we do know is that no one on their death bed has ever been quoted as wondering: "What if I had spent more time in the office?"

Let us turn now to the challenge of how our **ABCs** tool kit can help us in saying goodbye to other than a fleeting relationship.

Parting words

The moments alone that two loved ones share when one of them is about to pass on are also pregnant and alive with new possibilities. For one of them, the future holds a certain transition. A spirit, a soul, is about to be freed from its current bodily home. For the other, the future holds the need to grieve, as their own soul comes to terms with the loss of a loved one. These painful moments happen in all of our lives. We are powerless to alter the final outcome. The best we can hope for is that both of our souls can pass on to the next phase of our lives healed of any old scars. An example of how a few words can achieve this gift of healing follows below.

My mother died of a cancerous brain tumour. For weeks on end, she would lie completely comatose in her hospital bed in Tampa, Florida. It got to be that the nurses knew when I'd arrived in the lobby for my monthly visit from Boston. As soon as I did, my mother would open her eyes in anxious anticipation ... four floors above. Our unhealthy co-dependent relationship had deep roots. For much of our lives, we had lived under the constant threat of physical violence from my father, so we had learned to feel overly protective of the other.

Most of what I did over a several month period was simply *Attend*. I don't recall the many one-way conversations we had into the wee hours of the morning. I'll never forget the final one. It was 4:30 a.m. and I had just awakened from a few moments of exhausted shut-eye. As I looked up at her face, I could see her eyes, opened wide, locked in on me. I recognised that look immediately. It was the same one any loving concerned parent would manifest towards one of our children when they were infants lying in their cribs. Stealing a peek at them, just to make sure they were okay.

I stood and lifted my mother's now 5st 5lb body into my arms. Smiling, I leaned over and kissed her parched lips. Then, as our souls met in nonverbal communion, I said, "It's okay, mom. You can go. I can take care of myself now."

She returned my smile. A tear rolled down her cheek. She closed her eyes for the last time.

That one interaction did not heal me forever of the many scars I endured as a child growing up. I still had (and have) a lot to work through to free myself of the bondage of my past. However, like Shaya's experience on the ball field, my mother's gift to me was a heart-felt nonverbal silent *Appreciate:* the smile on "her parched lips". My gifts to her were a confident *Describe:* "It's okay, mom" followed by two compassionate *Prescribes,* promises of assurance that "I can take care of myself now … You can go". These few words opened a door and allowed a ray of sunshine and hope to bathe both of our souls. We were freed to move on.

The seasons of our lives

For a variety of obvious reasons, longer interactions between loved ones in their final moments are not readily available. The forest in which Bambi [17] roamed, however, provides us with an example rich in additional insights as to how our **ABCs** can make a final moment—indeed, any moment—one in which our Higher Power speaks to us.

> The leaves were falling from the great oak at the meadow's edge. They were falling from all the trees. One branch of the oak reached high above the others and stretched far out over the meadows. Two leaves clung to its very tip.
>
> "It isn't the way it used to be," said one leaf to the other.
>
> "No," the other leaf answered. "So many of us have fallen off tonight, we're almost the only ones left on the branch."
>
> "You never know who is going to go next," said the first leaf. "Even when it was warm and the sun shone, a storm or a cloudburst would come sometimes, and many leaves were torn off, though they were still young. You never know who's going to go next."

"The sun seldom shines now," sighed the second leaf, "and when it does it gives no warmth. We must have warmth again."

"Can it be true," said the first leaf, "can it really be true, that others come to take our places when we're gone and after them still others, and more and more?"

"It is really true," whispered the second leaf. "We can't even begin to imagine it, it's beyond our powers."

"It makes me very sad," added the first leaf.

They were silent a while. Then the first leaf said quietly to herself "Why must we fall? ... "

The second leaf asked "What happens to us when we have fallen?"

"We sink down ...."

"What is under us?"

The first leaf answered, "I don't know. Some say one thing, some another, but nobody knows."

The second leaf asked, "Do we feel anything. Do we know anything about ourselves when we're down there?"

The leaf answered, "Who knows? Not one of all those down there has ever come back to tell us about it."

They were silent again. Then the first leaf said tenderly to the other "Don't worry so much about it, you're trembling."

"That's nothing," the second leaf answered. "I tremble at the least thing now. I don't feel so sure of my hold as I used to."

"Let's not talk any more about such things," said the first leaf.

The other replied "No, we'll let it be. But, what else shall we talk about?" She was silent, but went on after a little while. "Which one of us will go first?"

"There's still plenty of time to worry about that," the other leaf assured her. "Let's remember how beautiful it was, how wonderful, when the sun came out and shone so warmly that we thought we'd burst with life. Do you remember? And the morning dew, and the mild and splendid nights ...."

We can easily personalise these passages. Two old friends, sitting at the edge of a dock, fishing rods in hand reminiscing about life. Numerous reflective *Push Describes*—"So many of us have fallen off ..." "The sun seldom shines now ..."—are interspersed with *Pull Asks* that are most often relegated to the heart and seldom voiced—"What happens to us when we have fallen?" "What is under us?" "Do we feel anything ...?"

Neither party presumed to Push definitive responses to these imponderables upon the other. Nor was there any judging going on—"Oh silly, everyone knows that ..." Rather, the questions either got the *Pull*ing power of *Attend*—"They were silent again"—or a simple *Describe*—"I don't know ... Nobody knows". When two hearts share the inherent ambiguity and uncertainty of life, a strong common bond is forged.

As this bond of mutual comfort, understanding and love forms, there is an even deeper sharing that takes place. Each begins to *Describe* heretofore undisclosed facts locked in their hearts: "I don't feel so sure of my hold as I used to". Indeed, the passage closes with an attempt to lighten the emotional load with an *Inspire*. The rekindling of a picture of "how beautiful it was, how wonderful ... that we thought we'd burst with life". An attempt, it turned out, did not immediately have the desired consequence.

> "Now the nights are dreadful," the second leaf complained, "and there's no end to them."
>
> "We shouldn't complain," said the first leaf gently. "We've outlived many, many others."
>
> "Have I changed much?" asked the second leaf, shyly but determinedly.
>
> "Not the least," the first leaf assured her. "You only think so because I've gone so yellow and ugly. But it's different in your case."
>
> "You're fooling me," the second leaf said.
>
> "No, really, you're as lovely as the day you were born. Here and there maybe a little yellow spot but it's hardly noticeable and makes you handsomer, believe me."
>
> "Thanks," whispered the second leaf, quite touched. "I don't believe you, not all together, but I thank you because you're so kind, you've always been so kind to me. I'm just beginning to understand how kind you are."
>
> "Hush," said the other leaf, and kept silent herself for she was too troubled to talk any more.
>
> They were both silent. Hours passed.
>
> A moist wind blew, cold and hostile, through the tree tops.
>
> "Ah, now," said the second leaf, "I ...". Then her voice broke off. She was torn from her place and spun down.
>
> Winter had come.

What courage it took for the second leaf to *Ask* "determinedly, 'Have I changed much?'" The first leaf demonstrated its sensitivity to the more direct concern which lay "shyly" unexpressed behind this question: "Am I still beautiful to you? Do you still love me?" In an attempt to make things right and deny the truth, the first leaf *Describes* two absolutes: "Not the least" and "You only think so because I've gone so yellow and ugly".

However well-intentioned, the second leaf refused to be placated— "You're fooling me". The first leaf was then forced to come more to the truth with a relative *Describe*: "Here and there maybe a little yellow spot ...", and a sincere believable *Appreciate*: "and makes you handsomer, believe me". In return for this honesty with compassion, the second leaf affirmed a gift of *Appreciation* that heretofore had also gone unrecognised: "You're so kind, you've always been so kind to me. I'm just beginning to understand how kind you are".

Consequently, the two leaves were able to keep "saying hello hello hello" each and every moment of their lives together, until it was time to "say goodbye ... to say go go go" to their lives together. In staying fully present to the moment, in saying hello to each and every new passing moment, they carried the warmth of each other's comfort, understanding and love in their hearts into the cold winter of their lives.

As we stand moment to moment on the uncertain threshold of the winter of our lives, our rides in taxis, our walks along the beach and through the forest, leave us with the challenge of several poignant questions. Can we age with grace, courage and humility? Can we be comfortable in our own and each other's silence? Do we have the courage to admit our innermost fears and uncertainties to another human being?

And, perhaps, most importantly, can we look back over our lives, and its many relationships, and answer yes to questions like:

In my own fallible fumbling way, did I speak to my loved ones every day as if they were the last words heard from my heart?

Did I treat every moment as if it was a first hello and a final goodbye?

Chapter Ten

Discourse of the silent variety

"Life consists of what man is thinking of all day."

(Emerson)

"The only tyrant I accept in this world is the still small voice within me."

(Gandhi)

IMAGINE BEING bombarded as a child in subtle and not-so-subtle terms with messages from parents such as: "You're stupid and will never amount to anything". While your parents may have long since passed on, these messages become recorded tapes sitting patiently in a pause mode. At the mere flick of a switch, they will rise to rob our souls of the self-esteem needed to live our lives to their fullest.

Once these self-defeating behaviours become habitual and reflexive, our conscious minds place the internal voices into the background. But, in spite of the fact that the mute button has been engaged, the actions taking place on the screens of our mind remain unchanged. We act *as if* a negative internal voice, of which we are consciously unaware, is guiding our actions. When asked: 'Why did you do that? You know how bad it is for you" we look as puzzled as those who are frustrated with us. We intuitively know we are exhibiting behaviours that are harmful to us, particularly when stressed. But we don't know why. The stress seems to justify the action. We feel helpless to do anything different. This built-in self-protective capacity makes uncovering and changing their patterns even more challenging.

Consequently, the life we enact on the world stage is a reflection of the tens of thousands of private screenings playing in the theatres of our minds. Each of these screenings contains a cast of "bad guys" representing the negative self-images that others have planted into our minds. However, while they may take on a variety of seemingly different roles, the important fact is that it is our name that appears in the credits as writer, director, leading actor, supporting actress. We are both the speaker and listener to the most important discourse that ever takes place in our lives. Therefore, the win-win quality of what we project unto our audiences—the people with whom we interact—is driven, in large part, by the win-win quality of our self-talk.

If our **ABC**s can help a Higher Power speak to us through other people, can the **ABC**s be applied to help us turn these internal dialogues into opportunities to speak to our inner selves as our Higher Power would? The answer to this question is an emphatic *Yes!* As a result, we can learn to confront the demons, the "bad guys" lurking in the shadows of our own souls. Doing so will allow us to stop projecting these internal demons onto others and, thereby, strengthen our opportunities for having it both ways.

Tuning into internal dialogues, disengaging our mute buttons—and, where need be, altering the dialogues taking place—will challenge us. In return for facing this struggle, we are given a vital key to opening up our hearts and achieving the harmonious relationships we seek, with ourselves and others. Our animal friends can help us to see this truth, as the following story affirms:

To be(e) or not to be(e)

Several years ago, I had the occasion to spend eight days in total silence at a Buddhist meditation retreat. Waking hours were spent in two primary activities, each 45 minutes in length: sitting in the traditional lotus position or walking back-and-forth over a 25 yard path I'd been given as my turf for the retreat.

My first time down that stretch of earth brought me face-to-face with a huge black carpenter bee. While ominous in size and colour, these bees—unlike their yellow-jacketed cousins—are known not to sting humans, preferring instead to bore into the shingles of homes. These facts were irrelevant. As a result of some abusive childhood experiences, I had an obsessive phobia about bees. As a youngster I used to stomp on any and every bee I ran across. As an adult, I matured a bit. I chose to merely run in the opposite direction every time I encountered a bee. Here I was not only unable to run, but also expected to learn to walk painstakingly slowly and peacefully on a path owned by an arch enemy.

Eight days later—full of serenity and loving kindness for all of God's creatures—I began my last mediation walk. No sooner did my foot hit the path, than the bee—as it had done periodically during the week—buzzed around my head. In what I can only describe as an out-of-body-like experience, I tried to muster every learning I'd gleaned from the week. From a detached perspective, I consciously tried to change my normal blasphemous thoughts about my enemy. I simply noted my fear, disappointment, anxiety, and—if you'll pardon the pun—tried to just let it "bee".

For the next 45 minutes, that bee sat perched upon my right shoulder. When the chimes sounded signalling the end of my walk, I stood motionless. The bee lifted off my shoulder, flew around my head several times, and then took off. I have no idea where it went, but I do know my phobia of bees went with it.

The language of the heart

What is remarkable about that experience is how unremarkable it is. Since the beginning of time, indigenous people have accepted that an animal's senses are remarkably attuned to the feelings and motives harboured in our hearts and the thoughts they generate in our minds. Young children whose natural growth and being have not yet been blocked by adult rules are thought to be equally sensitive to very subtle nuances.

When our motives are pure, when with our every action towards them we grant them the same access to "life, liberty, and the pursuit of happiness" as we seek for ourselves, animals can be our best friends. To be sure, not all animals—no more than all human beings—can be completely and implicitly trusted. Betrayal is a part of life. Sound judgement in the present moment—not prejudgement, the sound of pre-recorded internal tapes—is called for in all of our relationships. Yet, when we choose to think badly about, talk down to, and act unkindly towards some of our best friends (or ourselves) as if they were "dumb animals", we seem confused as to why they hiss, snarl, and strike out at us.

J. Allen Boone, in his book *Kinship With All* Life [18] about his many experiences of having it both ways with the world of animals, explains it this way: "the most effective way to achieve right relations with any living thing is to look for the best in it and then help that best to the fullest expression". Boone's and many other similar documented experiences confront us with poignant questions about our approach to relationships.

If the less developed animal world is tuned into messages radiating from our hearts and minds, can we continue to deny that same power exists in our more developed human relationships? Are we prepared to accept the fact that unspoken *Pushes* and *Pulls*—our internal dialogues—have as much of an impact on our relationship with ourselves as our external spoken dialogues have on others? Are we prepared "to look for the best" in ourselves, and "then help that best to [its] fullest expression?"

Our self-talk has the power to defeat us or assist in the expression of what is best in us. The early signs of the self-defeating cycle are familiar. At some point in our lives, we suffer a disappointment, a setback, a severe loss. Things seem not to be going our way. A committee meeting begins to rage in our minds. Pointed ascriptions—should haves, could haves and accusatory fingers of blame—flood our conscious thoughts. Reasonable *Prescribes—I suggest ... You might consider ...*—and balanced *Appreciates—The good parts were ... The parts that could be better were ...*—are nowhere to be heard.

For the moment, suffice to say that if someone else talked to us in the way many of us talk to ourselves, we would not *Attend* to them for long. We would turn them off in a flash.

To salve this self-inflicted attack on our self-esteem, the seductive doors of self-pity invite us to visit. All we have to do to receive a dose of comfort and understanding is be willing to accept the role of victim for a moment. "Poor me!" voiced to others will regularly get the desired response of "Poor you!".

Frequent visits to this enticing swamp create a well-worn path with steep sides. Many of us fall headlong into it even before we are aware that we've got close! Before we know it, a short visit rapidly takes on the dynamics of traditional addictions. A voice in our minds tells us that to feel comfort, understanding, and love we need only take a quick fix—food, drink, sex, smoking—or engage in some retail therapy—go shopping. "I deserve it!" "With all I've been through, who could blame me?" "What the heck, I can start my diet tomorrow".

The land of false promises turns into a bottomless pit. Every struggle to fight our way out seems only to send us deeper into a black abyss. Every failed attempt to pull ourselves up robs us of another measure of self-esteem.

Depression sets in. We stop fighting. Wallowing is easier than changing. Powerless to do anything to help ourselves relieve this miserable feeling, we start exhibiting behaviours towards others that decrease their ability to help. We feel truly miserable. In our misery, we act like misers.

We begin by begrudgingly parting with comfort, understanding, and love others may need. We give less. Sooner or later, others begin to reduce their emotional investment in us accordingly. As a consequence, we get more resentful at feeling even less comforted, understood, and loved by them. The withholding tax of conditional exchanges—"If I do xxx, then you'll have to do yyy"—increases. Having it both ways turns into a lose-lose war of attrition versus a win-win partnership of appreciation.

Not a pretty picture by any means. One, it has been estimated, that over 25 million Americans alone see in their mind's eye and feel in their hearts regularly. Depression medications are only a partial solution. Because the root cause of the dis-ease is relationship-based—beginning with significant others and carried forward in our memory banks—real mending must also be relationship-based.

Making up our minds to change the make-up of our minds

In looking at how the nature of our internal dialogues and our intra-personal relationships contribute to such chronic depression, we will be utilising truths and their consequences comparable to those we touched upon earlier with respect to our interpersonal relationships. Let us review them quickly.

Just as every behaviour we exhibit, intentional or otherwise, has a consequence, every conversation we have in our minds affects the make up of our minds. Choosing to dwell on an internal thought is a precursor to an external action. The thoughts we attend to in our minds are among the most powerful mind-altering substances we know.

Repeatedly exhibiting the same behaviour towards another person and expecting different consequences is foolish. Similarly, if we keep talking to ourselves the same way, we'll keep getting identical results. In the world of Einstein's relativity and Newton's laws of motion, every action may cause an equal and opposite reaction. But in the world of interpersonal relationships, our reactions to others are more often equal than opposite to our feelings towards ourselves. Conversations with ourselves devoid of comfort, understanding, and love breed self-contempt. Their opposites build self-esteem. How we think, feel, and talk to ourselves will influence how we think, feel, and talk to others. "What goes around, comes around".

If a relationship is not yielding the win-win consequences we desire, it is our responsibility and accountability to focus on how we might change our behaviour to effect a different consequence. The challenge can be daunting when we are face-to-face with a significant other. It pales by comparison to the situation of self-talk, when the face looking back at us is our own!

How are we to implement the 100%-50% truth when the relationship we are talking about is how we go about relating to ourselves? When we make up both halves of the relationship? Can we actually make up our minds to change the make up of our minds?

We believe the answer is *Yes*. The images in our minds, for example, may clearly resemble and sound like our parents. But, at this moment, they are nothing more than images. We are—to re-emphasise a point made earlier—individually, the writers, directors, actors, and actresses of the dramas taking place on the stages of our minds. Let's take a look at how the rewriting process might proceed by using a real experience.

Several back-to-back business setbacks had seriously eroded my sense of self-confidence and optimism. A protective dike was needed against what I knew was an incoming tide of the negative self-talk, magnetically attracted to any smell of fear. When others have a problem and seek help, my overdeveloped behavioural instinct is to lead with future-oriented *Push* energies, *Prescribes* and *Inspires*. Because I usually exhibit the same habit towards myself, my initial internal dialogue was predictable. I chose to increase my use of internal *Push* energy with stronger *Prescribes*— "I *will* get the next contract!"—and/or visualisations of success using more intense *Inspires*—"Imagine how *incredibly sweet* it will be to bask in the glow of victory!"

While engaging in this attempt to drown out the early rumblings of my negative self-defeating thoughts, I know *they*, my degrading internal dialogues, are there in the wings. Doing push-ups to stay in shape. Patiently awaiting their cue to rush centre stage. I mean to speak of them, *they*, as if they were living breathing beings. They are parts of the totality that is me.

If circumstances were such that I experienced an early business success, my self-confidence and optimism would be quickly restored. My debasing internal tapes know that. They are frighteningly patient and waiting on pause for yet another chance to erode my self-esteem.

When the external pattern continues, as it did recently, I get tired of trying to boost my spirits with these inspiring visualisations and assertive prescriptions. The volume of my efforts at this form of self-bolstering begins to fade. Self-defeating voices lick their chops and rush to the fore to begin their familiar chorus.

A sampling of the most frequent of these thoughts would include:

- Why don't I just give up!
- I should have known better than to even try!
- What a colossal fool I am!
- There's no way I can turn this one around!
- How could I be so stupid!
- That'll teach me to get my hopes up!

(To get a sense of how these might sound if *someone else* were voicing them to you, substitute *You* ... or *You are* ... for *I am* ... or ... *me*. Then ask yourself how long you would tolerate such verbal abuse!)

At this point, I have to be very cautious. I'm prone to make the same mistake with these inner voices as I would if another person expressed similar words, music, and dance towards me. Namely, I need to resist the temptation to waste my energies in a *Push-Push* internal mental debate.

> What a colossal fool I am!
> No I'm not!
> Yes you are!
> Prove it!
> Well, isn't this the third time you made this mistake?
> Yeah, but if it hadn't been for ...
> Yeah, but if you'd listened to me in the first place, you'd never ...

Constantly using exclusively *Push* energies, whether it is two different people arguing with each other or one person arguing with him or herself, results in the same outcome. Like fighting with a tar baby, the more you struggle, the more tied up you get. Until you just quit out of exhaustion.

Another school of thought would have us believe that we need simply to substitute positive affirmations, *positive Appreciates*, for negative self-talk statements, *negative Appreciates*. "I am a very successful person!" instead of "What a colossal fool I am!" Or "I am very intelligent!" versus "How could I be so stupid!" While such outpourings of praise can do no harm, they are unlikely to have a lasting positive impact. Again, I'll use myself as an example.

My father was a very competitive perfectionist. When I'd bring home a high school test with a score of 95, his first question would be "What happened to the other 5 points?" When I'd get a score of 100, he'd wonder if the test had been too simple, or how many others got the same grade. No matter what I did, it was never enough. Being a perfectionist, and overly hard on myself with self-talk, was a language I understood ... and still do!

Consequently, self-esteem (self-interest bearing accounts) in my soul—those that might otherwise have stored up self-affirming experiences for subsequent withdrawal on rainy days—were generally depleted. Years of verbal abuse heaped upon me, first by my father and then by myself, had burned huge holes in the protective shield of my self-esteem. I imagined it looked like a sieve. Whenever anyone poured concentrated praise upon me, or I tried to pour it on myself, it ran out and immediately became diffused and diluted. Until these holes were healed from the inside out, simple positive self-affirmations were not going to be of long-term value.

Our negative self-talk won't be easily pushed away. Nor will it succumb to logical debate. Like a frightened or spoiled child, neither will it be ignored or walked away from. No matter how hard we push ourselves, how fast we run the rat race of life, we cannot pull away from our own shadows. Liane Cordes puts it this way: "It is not enough to 'will away' our dissatisfactions. Fighting our past only brings it upon us. Until we learn to surrender to our imperfections and admit our limitations, we cannot receive new insight and understanding ...."

What alternatives remain to surrendering to, giving in to, not giving up on, these tapes we all carry around?

Becoming a third party observer

We believe the answer comes from stepping outside of ourselves for a moment. Ask yourself the following question: What would you hope to do if someone you love shares things with you about how they are thinking or feeling about themselves like the following:

- Why don't I just give up!
- I should have known better than to even try!
- What a colossal fool I am!
- There's no way I can turn this one around!
- How could I be so stupid!
- That'll teach me to get my hopes up!

The answer is obvious. You'd make every effort to use all of the *Push* and *Pull* win-win behavioural skills in your **ABCs** tool kit to engage this person in a dialogue that hopefully leaves them feeling more comforted, understood, and loved. You'd try to be the best friend you know how to be.

In a similar vein, if all other efforts fail to make our self-talk less self-defeating, the only remaining alternative is to struggle to make friends with these voices. In the process of struggling to deepen our friendship with our self-talk, we get to comfort, understand, and ultimately love our deeper selves—our souls. Engaging in this uncommon dialogue offers us the opportunity to develop the friendship with *the* God that resides in each and every one of our souls.

This is not as hard or strange as it might at first sound. Unless they've become completely muted into our unconscious, we are aware these conversations are taking place in our minds. Even if we don't hear them directly, the behaviours they trigger warn us we are acting *as if* we'd been spoken to in a certain way or tone of voice. Our challenge is to use this **A**wareness consciously and choose an alternative set of **B**ehaviours with which to engage our negative self-talk in order to effect a more positive lasting win-win outcome as a **C**onsequence. We will use our behavioural **ABC**s on ourselves, to make friends with our selves.

A written format is one way to portray this dialogue. A snapshot of how this process might work and where it can potentially lead, follows.

The sanity of talking to your self

The critical voices I most often hear are echoes of those my father initially implanted so I'll substitute *You* for *I*. In other words, the *Push-Pull* dialogue I'm trying to create is between my memory of him (F = his voice) and a new, more comforting, understanding, loving side of me than the angry finger-pointing *Push-Push* debate noted above (I = my new responses).

(F) "What a colossal fool you are. How could you be so stupid!"

(I) "You sound really angry and disappointed in me. *(Empathise)* What have I done to deserve that?" *(Ask)*

(F) "I didn't send you to M.I.T. to make those kinds of mistakes."

(I) "So you feel that it was a mistake to support my education? Is that what you're saying?" *(Understand)*

(F) "You know very well why I made sure you went to college!"

(I) "You've said so I'd never have to work with my hands like you did." *(Describe)*

(F) "You got that right. If I'd been able to go to a fancy college, I wouldn't have had to work with my hands all my life."

(I) "It must have been hell as a teenager to be supporting your entire family. *(Empathise)* I wish you'd been able to go to college, too." *(Describe)* [My father's father died suddenly when my father was only 14 years old.]

(F) "Yeah, well that's water under the bridge."

(I) "Well, I am sorry and I am very grateful for your support. *(Appreciate)*

(F) "I, uh, I, uh, know you are, I guess. Look, I don't mean to be unkind. I just want you to succeed."

(I) "I do too. I'm doing the best that I can. *(Describe)* And I know you did the best you could, as well." *(Appreciate)*

(F) "Well it wasn't good enough, was it? (Quiet pause.) I feel pretty stupid myself sometimes."

(I) "Welcome to the human race. *(Empathy)* Wanna compare notes?" *(Ask)*

Before a word about how the entire dialogue turned out, let us take a moment and note the choices I was consciously making to try to change my part in this conversation. The internal dialogue above reflects numerous attempts at comfort, understanding, and even love. They are not intended to be prescribes to the dialogue that another person might find healing in their own circumstances, but rather to simply demonstrate a process.

I tried to resist the temptation to defensively *Push* back, my typical reaction to one of his barbs. Before reacting, I carefully thought about alternatives. As a result, I made a conscious attempt to *Pull* much more: to *Understand, Empathise,* and *Ask*. When I did allow myself to *Push* back, I tried to stress positive *Appreciates* that were sincere: "I am sorry". "I know you did the best you could, as well". "I am very grateful for your support". I also have to read the dialogue aloud (in my case, with the help of a counsellor) so I can hear and experience the full range of my feelings. (Readers will have to adapt this process to fit their own styles and motivations. But, getting the dialogues out of our minds, by writing them down or using an audio machine, is vital to helping stop them from driving us out of our minds!)

There is no doubt in my mind that my father's spontaneous softening and self-disclosure was a direct result of me changing my part of our self-talk: "I feel pretty stupid myself sometimes" (an example of a *Describe*) Of course, he didn't really say those words. Nor does my attempt to alter our internal dialogue negate or deny the validity of my pain in growing up with him. But, by taking 100% responsibility for my 50% of our relationship, for my part of the conversation, I could perhaps live the rest of my life differently. Perhaps I could draw strength from the gifts he was able to share with me, gifts that would otherwise remain distorted by the broken record of resentment and bitterness that played in my mind.

If I couldn't change this internal pattern, my old external pattern would continue. Every time I'd experience success, my ability to enjoy and savour it would be short-lived. My self-talk would depreciate my accomplishments and widen the holes in my self-esteem sieve even further.

How could I lose by striving to create a collaborative win-win dialogue instead of a competitive lose-lose diatribe?

So what happened? My father was, in fact, a very successful entrepreneur who lost everything he had due to some very poor personal and business decisions. As our internal dialogue continued, the focus shifted dramatically to our talking about the mistakes and successes in both of our lives. Both of us began to use a balance of *Push* and *Pull*. Describes were followed by Appreciates and Empathy or Asks that deepened the disclosure. Silent periods of Attending were not sources of discomfort but opportunities for deeper reflection. Real and imagined truths, long walled behind a dike of denial, flooded forth. Buried resentments surfaced and were partially healed by laughter and tears.

As a result of this process, a major shift in acceptance and tolerance took place. Rays of sunshine began to warm the otherwise cold memory of my father who had died several years before this internal conversation took place. I came to realise that I was holding myself back because I didn't want to defeat my father and make him feel badly! If I surpassed him any further, I'd lose him forever. But to not strive to fulfil my utmost potential was to lose myself forever. Because parents and children are inextricably linked to one another, there was no way we could rid ourselves of the other without killing our souls. We had no choice but to deepen our friendship and reduce our competitiveness. The law of all relationships, as Auden puts it, is to "Love each other or perish".

Is it the final chapter? No. Having had the experience of this new dialogue will not forever heal a long-term relationship scarred by self-doubt, fear, self-criticism, and a lack of confidence. We are mortal human beings, not Gods. Progress not perfection is our lot in life.

Liane Cordes puts it this way: "When we are filled with self-doubt, very few of us can muster the courage or confidence necessary to face even the most ordinary of events. Moreover, our self-doubt often makes us question the very purpose of our lives. Although we may try to overcome our lack of self-confidence by sheer self-propulsion, too often our efforts result in exhaustion and despair. Then it is almost impossible to shut out the hundreds of additional doubts and fears that run rampant in our fatigued minds .... One sure cure for our lack of self-confidence is faith in ... our Greatest Friend, Ally, and Support."

Call it what we will—Higher Power, God, soul, spirit—there is an inner force within us that wants only the very best for us. Each time circumstances bring self-defeating voices to the fore, we are given another opportunity to consciously insert into our internal dialogue the voice of a Being who is unconditionally comforting, understanding, and loving. Abraham Lincoln relied heavily on the freedom and courage afforded his soul in doing what it knew was right by such a deep friendship: "Without the assistance of a Divine Being ... I cannot succeed. With that assistance, I cannot fail."

Communing with this voice, the God within each of us, gives us the opportunity to learn how to better comfort, understand, and love our imperfect selves.

In so doing, we are strengthened in our ability to similarly improve our "kinship with all life", even those of our enemies.

When these enemies, these demons, happen to reside in our own hearts and minds, it is doubly important that we learn to make friends with them.

In these cases, *them* is *us*.

A win-win outcome is assured.

We end up having it both ways.

Chapter Eleven

When you must burn
a bridge behind you

"Tie two birds together. They will not be able to fly, even though they now
have four wings."

T HE **ABCs** tool kit has proven its versatility across a diversity of
situations. Sensitive use of our Behavioural Compass has pointed
the way to increasing the frequency of those moments when we
know something special has taken place. The situations we've examined
have been far-reaching. We learned how not to repeat the experiences of
a stag and his son when they allowed themselves to live a life full of bitterness, devoid of the deep love and respect they actually felt for one
another. Fleeting moments with strangers in taxicabs were shown to be
equally rich opportunities to *do what love would do* as encounters in
the kitchen with intimate partners. Rather than proving to be a sign of
questionable sanity, talking to ourselves in a win-win manner emerged
as a sure-fire way to improve our sense of lucidity. And, as I experienced
with my mother, even the finality of death affords us the chance to use
our **ABCs** tool kit to mutual advantage and as an opportunity for
mutual growth.

Against this backdrop of spiritual hope, many readers have experienced (and may still be experiencing) an intimate relationship whose
reality is the exact opposite of something special. Instead of the heaven
on earth ideal we've tried to paint, many are caught in a relationship
whirlpool sucking them forever downward into a cesspool of living hell.

Instead of seeing the infinity of possibilities a blue sky provides, they
regularly feel more like the moth we described being swallowed by a
hungry bird. Rather than acting like an orange sunburst warming their
souls, the dawning of each new day in their relationship envelops them

in the blackness of despair. And, when their intimate other returns from a long trip and does remember to bring a surprise gift, it is likely to be embedded with a barbed hook.

Many are living in the iron grips of lose-lose co-dependent relationships. Fear and low self-esteem keep abused spouses coming back for more. Shame fuels self-defeating protective loyalty of their abusers. This negative spiral is not relegated solely to dis-eased co-dependent relationships with other human beings. Addicts relate to their intimate drugs of choice in the same manner ... with the same soul-killing consequences.

If our **ABCs** tool kit can show us the path to win-win, mutually advantageous and growth producing relationships, can it also be a light at the end of a lose-lose tunnel of despair? Can our Behavioural Compass help us to detect the early signs of a budding co-dependency? Are there *Push* and *Pull* tools that will enable us to protect, and, where need be, disconnect ourselves from lose-lose co-dependent relationships?

The story which follows will give us needed insights into how the **ABCs** can help when you must burn a bridge behind you.

The bridge

There was a man who had given much thought to what he wanted from life. He had experienced many moods and trials. He had experimented with different ways of living, and he had his share of success and failure. At last, he began to see clearly where he wanted to go.

Diligently, he searched for the right opportunity. Sometimes he came close, only to be pushed away. Often, he applied all his strength and imagination, only to find the path hopelessly blocked. And then at last it came. But the opportunity would not wait. If it were seen that he was not committed, the opportunity would not come again.

Eager to arrive, he started on his journey. With each step, he wanted to move faster; with each thought about his goal, his heart beat quicker; with each vision of what lay ahead, he found renewed vigour. Strength that had left him since his early youth returned, and desires, all kinds of desires, reawakened from their long-dormant positions.

Hurrying along, he came upon a bridge that crossed through the middle of town. It had been built high above a river in order to protect it from the floods of spring.

He started across. Then he noticed someone coming from the opposite direction. As they moved closer, it seemed as though the other was coming to greet him. He could see clearly, however, that he did not know this other, who was dressed similarly except for something tied around his waist.

When they were within hailing distance, he could see that what the other had about his waist was a rope. It was wrapped around him many times and probably, if extended, would reach a length of 30 feet.

The other began to uncurl the rope, and, just as they were coming close, the stranger said: "Pardon me, would you be so kind as to hold the end a moment?"

Surprised by this politely phrased but curious request, he agreed without a thought, reached out, and took it.

"Thank you," said the other, who then added: "Two hands now, and remember, hold tight." Whereupon, the other jumped off the bridge.

Let us pause for a moment. Embedded in these first paragraphs are insights into the circumstances that can impact our vulnerability to co-dependent relationships. As our traveller began his vision quest, he sensed "the opportunity would not come again". Little wonder "desires, all kinds of desires, reawakened from their long-dormant positions".

When our calling in life speaks to us with undeniable clarity, it is as if a deeply rooted dream has been awakened. Our souls come alive with "renewed vigour". Our hearts "beat quicker". And, at the same time that this orange ball of fire is bursting into our lives, unresolved black storm clouds show up in stark relief. The brighter is the sun which shines on a soul, the larger is the shadow which is cast. The success of our journey will be dependent upon the courage we can muster to deal with the dark sides of our shadows. For in these shadows lurk the internal self-defeating dialogues, to which we referred in the last chapter, waiting patiently in the wings, doing push ups to stay in shape.

Our traveller proved to be as vulnerable as the fly to the spider. His own intuition "Surprised by this politely phrased but curious request …" was clouded by his singularity of purpose. "He agreed, *without a thought*" to reach out and take the loose end of a 30 foot rope wrapped around a total stranger's waist.

"Pardon me, would you be so kind as to hold this end for a moment?" appeared to be a seductively innocuous *Pull—Ask*. The *Appreciate* of a "Thank you …" was followed by the urgency of a *Prescribe* "… two hands now, and remember, hold tight".

What's missing from this conversation? A powerful clue that a co-dependency is in the offing is the absence of any attempt at a two-way dialogue. Our vision-seeker did not *Pull* after the politely phrased but curious, out-of-the-blue request. No checking *Understanding*. No *Ask*ing for more explanations. Nor did the other signal what he was going to do and *Ask* for feedback, before the fact of taking action. These are some of the kinds of clues that someone is likely to be left holding the bag.

Now that the hook has been set, let us return to our story.

Quickly, the free-falling body hurtled the distance of the rope's length, and from the bridge the man abruptly felt the pull. Instinctively, he held tight and was almost himself dragged over the side. He managed to brace himself against the edge, however, and after having caught his breath, looked down at the other dangling, close to oblivion.

"What are you trying to do?" he yelled.

"Just hold tight," said the other.

"This is ridiculous," the man thought and began trying to haul the other in. He could not get the leverage, however. It was as though the weight of the other person had been carefully calculated in advance so that together they created a counterweight.

"Why did you do this?" the man cried out.

"I am your responsibility, " said the other.

"Well, I did not ask for it, "the man said.

"If you let go, I am lost," repeated the other.

He began to look around for help. But there was no one. How long would he have to wait? Why did this happen to befall him now, just as he was on the verge of success? He examined the side, searching for a place to tie the rope. Some protrusion, perhaps, or maybe a hole in the boards. But the railing was unusually uniform in shape; there were no spaces between the boards. There was no way to get rid of this new-found burden, even temporarily.

"What do you want?" he asked the other hanging below.

"Just your help," the other answered.

"How can I help? I cannot pull you in, and there is no place to tie the rope so that I can go and find someone to help me help you."

"I know that. Just hang on; that will be enough. Tie the rope around your waist; it will be easier."

Fearing that his arms could not hold out much longer, he tied the rope around his waist.

"Why did you do this?" he asked again. "Don't you see what you have done? What possible purpose could you have had in mind?"

"Just remember," said the other, "my life is in your hands."

What should he do? "If I let go, all my life I will know that I let this other die. If I stay, I risk losing my momentum towards my own long-sought-after salvation. Either way this will haunt me forever." With ironic humour, he thought to die himself, instantly, to jump off the bridge while still holding on. "That would teach this fool." But he wanted to live and to live fully. "What a choice I have to make; how shall I ever decide?"

In co-dependent relationships, actions are "carefully calculated in advance". The motivation for doing so, however, is quite different from the careful consideration and sensitive use of the **ABCs** we've been recommending. The balance sought in a co-dependent relationship is purely selfish. The "counterweight" created is intended to keep the other a prisoner, by creating conditions "just beyond his strength" to alter the circumstances.

An abusive spouse must keep their partner in the relationship or the game is no fun! Similarly, periods of white-knuckle abstinence from drugs or alcohol are often the seductive prelude to even more damaging binges.

Coding the dialogue above provides clear signs how this is accomplished. When our traveller tries to *Pull* answers to vital questions— "What are you trying to do?" or "Why did you do this?"—no Describe answers are forthcoming. Instead, we see repeated use of *Prescribes*: "Just hold tight", "If you let go, I am lost", "Just remember, my life is in your hands". While we can assume the absence of any meaningful dance, it seems safe to imagine that the *Describe*: "I am your responsibility" might have been tinged with the music of guilt induction.

Our traveller finally gets a response to a *Pull Ask*—"What do you want?" The response he gets is a *Prescribe*, but not one that frees him from his bondage. Rather, it is one that ensures "it will be easier" to keep the game going: "Just your help". And, this, not freedom, not true problem-solving, is the goal of a co-dependent.

The truly insidious nature of co-dependency is that it saps us of our very life force. When we allow people, places and things to keep us from our calling, from nurturing our soul, the price is steep indeed. "With ironic humour, he thought to die himself, to jump off the bridge while still holding on." So blatant a lose-lose is this action, that suicide would be "logically justified" with the rationalisation it " ... would teach this fool".

Let us return to our story and see what happens as our traveller begins to reach the end of his rope.

> As time went by, still no one came. The critical moment of decision was drawing near. To show his commitment to his own goals, he would have to continue on his journey now. It was already almost too late to arrive in time. But what a terrible choice to have to make.
>
> A new thought occurred to him. While he could not pull this other up solely by his own efforts, if the other would shorten the rope from his end by curling it around his waist again and again, together they could do it. Actually, the other could do it by himself, so long as he, standing on the bridge, kept it still and steady.
>
> "Now listen," he shouted down. "I think I know how to save you." And he explained his plan.
>
> But the other wasn't interested.
>
> "You mean you won't help? But I told you I cannot pull you up myself, and I don't think I can hang on much longer either."
>
> "You must try," the other shouted back in tears. "If you fail, I die."
>
> The point of decision arrived. What should he do? "My life or the other's?" And then a new idea. A revelation. So new, in fact, it seemed heretical, so alien was it to his traditional way of thinking.

The tide is turning. Our traveller has come upon a potential win-win plan that will save his partner's life and allow his own journey to continue. He sends his own *Prescribe* warning shot across the bow: "I cannot pull you up myself, and I don't think I can hang on much longer either".

When the demons of co-dependency first sense the signals they are losing their strangle hold, their response is to withhold all *Push* and *Pull* energy: "But the other wasn't interested". When passive withdrawal fails to work, we see a return to *Prescribes*, complete with increased music and dance: "You must try," the other *shouted back in tears*. "If you fail, I die."

"And then a new idea. A revelation ... alien to his traditional way of thinking."

The 100%-50% rule comes to our traveller in this moment of decision.

> "I want you to listen carefully," he said, "because I mean what I am about to say. I will not accept the position of choice for your life, only for my own; the position of choice for your life, I hereby give back to you."
>
> "What do you mean?" the other asked, afraid.
>
> "I mean, simply, it's up to you. You decide which way this ends. I will become counterweight. You do the pulling and bring yourself up. I will even tug a little from here." He began unwinding the rope from around his waist and braced himself anew against the side.
>
> "You cannot mean what you say," the other shrieked. "You would not be so selfish. I am your responsibility. What could be so important that you would let someone die? Do not do this to me."
>
> He waited a moment. There was no change in the tension of the rope.
>
> "I accept your choice," he said, at last, and freed his hand.

There come times in our lives when we must burn a bridge behind us, when nothing short of a definitive *Prescribe* can free us from bondage: "I mean simply, it's up to you. You decide which way this ends". Standing up for ourselves, our souls, means we must resist the accusation that we are being so selfish.

To emphasise a comment made earlier: "To be self'ish—to be fully the person that we were created to be—is antithetical to selfishness. This *self in the service of us* is the essence of a true win-win relationship, of having it both ways".

Chapter Twelve

The hundredth monkey:
a leap of faith

T HIS STORY is true. Hard scientific data have confirmed the existence of energy fields, of awareness invisibly communicated from mind to mind, from heart to heart. Many refer to these powerful communications as God consciousness. Their scope ranges from the impact of prayer on healing to the ability of separated twins to tune into one another.

The Hundredth Monkey (Taken from the book of that title by
Ken Keyes, Jr.)
The Japanese monkey, Macaca fuscata, has been closely observed in the wild for a period of over 30 years. In 1952, on the island of Koshima, scientists were providing monkeys with sweet potatoes dropped in the sand. The monkeys liked the taste of the raw sweet potatoes but found the sandy dirt unpleasant.

An 18-month-old female named Imo found she could solve the problem by washing potatoes in a nearby stream. She taught this trick to her mother. Her playmates also learned this new way and they also taught their mothers.

This cultural innovation was gradually picked up by various monkeys before the eyes of the scientists. Between 1952 and 1958, all the young monkeys [on Koshima] learned to wash the sandy sweet potatoes to make them more palatable. Only the adults who imitated their children learned this social improvement while other adults kept eating the dirty sweet potatoes.

Then, in the autumn of 1958, something startling took place. A certain number of Koshima monkeys were washing sweet potatoes—the exact number is not known. Let us assume that when the sun rose one morning there were 99 monkeys on Koshima Island who had learned to wash their sweet potatoes. Later that morning, one more monkey [let's assume it was the hundredth] learned to wash potatoes.

THEN IT HAPPENED!

By that evening everyone in the tribe was washing sweet potatoes before eating them. The added energy of this "hundredth" monkey somehow created an ideological breakthrough.

But notice.

A most surprising thing was observed by these scientists: the habit of washing sweet potatoes then jumped over the sea! Colonies of monkeys on other islands and the Mainland troop of monkeys at Takasakiyama—who heretofore had endured the unpleasantness of the sand—began washing their sweet potatoes.

The hundredth monkey brings us full circle back to where our journey began, and forces us to rethink the truth of consequences. All behaviour, intentional or otherwise, has consequences. We are 100% accountable for the consequences of all of our behaviour, our 50% of any relationship. Therefore, the key factors to having it both ways—to win-win relationships—reside in our ABCs, an Awareness of our Behaviour and its Consequences.

We all enjoy the sweet taste that a good relationship leaves in our mouths. We'd prefer not to have to endure the dirt. As adults, however, we seldom follow the lead of our children and their playmates. On the other hand, we hope they will look to us, and not just to their peers, as their role models. As children, we had the same dilemma. Where could we look for answers to difficult choices between right and wrong but to our parents and peers? Where did our peers look? Where did our parents look? And so on, back to the beginning. So, understanding how we've got to where we are is not difficult.

According to the Bible, it began with Adam having to learn first how to relate to himself and all of God's other living creatures. Finding himself unsatisfied with just that relationship, Adam created an other with God's help. Then Adam and Eve faced the challenge of having to learn how to relate to one another. Cain and Abel learned their relationship skills from them. Cain, whose relationship skills were very suspect at best, as Abel would attest, added his own bits and pieces and passed them on to his progeny. And so on ....

At the most fundamental level, individuals are the basic building blocks of every social system, from families to businesses to cities to states to nations. In the business we call living, our interpersonal communications serve as a global net that encompasses all six billion of us.

Similar to a very complicated chemical compound, several trillion individual interpersonal relationship pairs stretch out to become our global community. When communication is working well between any two people, do we not often refer to that as *good chemistry?* When the process fails, several might feel the consequences. Employees will steer clear of a boss who has just been chewed out by another boss. Kindred to this, when two parents are continually at each other's throats, the children, and then their children, and then ... are adversely affected.

The mistakes of one generation affect the next generation, and the mess snowballs. Like many phenomena in nature, the consequences of poorly managed relationships grow exponentially.

Through our own conscious choices, guided by our own sense of morality, we determine the self-fulfilling or self-defeating nature of the social systems in which we live, learn, and work. Through the power to learn from our pasts, we can create better futures. Each of us has the power to preside as CEOs over our own lives and the business we call living. But we must start from where we are by first accepting the fact that what we've created is not a pretty picture.

No one is pleased with the familiar statistics about the human condition. We are afraid to walk in our polluted cities at night. Johnny can't read. Jill doesn't have a home. Jack's hooked on drugs. Nations are still building bombs. World governments continue to spend 60–70 times more on technologies of destruction than they do on education.

So, if our current situation is the cumulative result of the way any two people relate to one another, where will we be tomorrow? No one knows for sure. Alongside Biblical stories of creation, we have scientific matters of probabilities. Let's examine two end points along this probabilistic continuum.

The odds are ...

Scientist Stephen Hawking calculates that at one point in the development of the universe, before the "first big bang, the odds were *only* one-billionth of one-billionth of one percent that the conditions necessary for life would emerge on earth".

On the other hand, what are the probabilities that the conditions will emerge necessary for life on earth to end?

For three years during the early 1990s, General George Lee Butler, Commander-in-Chief of the US Strategic Command, was required to be no more than three rings away from his phone. His job? To execute an order from the President to use nuclear weapons. His answer to this question of probabilities is unequivocal: "The capacity for human error, human failure, mechanical failure, and *misunderstanding* was [is] <u>virtually infinite</u>." (Emphasis not in the original.)

Monkey see, monkey do

Between a "virtually infinite" capacity to have a misunderstanding that results in our "second—and final—'big bang'", and a probability of some "merely 80+ zeros" that life would ever emerge again on earth, lies the gift of our little 18-month-old monkey. We have two choices. Our next interpersonal encounter in this continuing chain reaction may result in a human failure, including most specifically a potentially lethal human misunderstanding. Or, we may see the beginning of a new set of human chain reactions that reflect our need to live in symbiotic harmony with all living creatures. Our choice may be a direct function of our willingness to ape the example of our primate relatives.

In her case, Imo couldn't do anything about her need for the sustenance of food. Nor can we, as we've stressed, do anything about the fact that we need regular helpings of emotional sustenance—comfort, understanding, and love. What Imo could do was exhibit a willingness to try something new when her needs were being frustrated. Can we afford to do any less?

The difference, of course, is that Imo was able to eliminate the dirt and increase the sweetness in her life by herself. She didn't need to collaborate with any of her brothers and sisters. We, on the other hand, must find mutually beneficial ways to alter the meat and potatoes of our human existence—the quality of our relationships—if our needs are to be met. In the game of life, a game we must all play together, win-lose is a mythical outcome.

We must wage peace until we all win, or we will most assuredly all lose.

It's as simple as ABC

In the preceding pages, we've tried to simplify this challenge down to its most basic steps. Having it both ways, enjoying the rewards of win-win relationships, requires that two people be committed to becoming parties to a continuous dynamic exchange process aimed at improving their ABCs: Awareness of their Behaviour and its Consequences.

A. We make an effort to increase our *Awareness*. We ask each other to specify in observable behavioural terms what we need from the other to feel comforted, understood, and loved.

B. We then do our best to deliver the *Behaviours* requested by the other person.

C. We monitor the *Consequences* of our behaviours by asking for feedback, which, in turn, further increases our *Awareness*, and so on.

So in closing, let's suppose that when the sun arose one morning, there were 98 "monkeys" on the Earth. Each had committed themselves to learning how to develop and maintain win-win relationships. Let's further suppose that later that morning a 99th "monkey" somewhere decided to reduce the interpersonal dirt and increase the interpersonal sweetness in its own life.

THEN IT HAPPENED.

"Then what happened? We're still one short!" you think.

Carl Jung noted that "the meeting of two personalities is like the contact of two chemical substances: If there is any reaction, both are transformed". To this Bell added: "animate objects, once having been in contact, *both* change if there is a subsequent change in the other, *no matter how far apart they are*".

Therefore, by accepting the truth that all of us are 100% accountable for the consequences of all of our behaviour—our 50% of any relationship —the 99th "monkey" has virtually guaranteed the emergence of the hundredth!

Such is the gift our Higher Power bestows upon us when we strive for having it both ways.

Appendix

Description of behaviours

Push behaviours

Describe

1. Clearly explain the bases for your decisions.
9. Use well-reasoned arguments to support your proposals.
17. Use well-reasoned arguments to support your counterproposals.
25. Use well-reasoned counterarguments when you disagree with others.
33. Openly provide others with information they might not normally have.
41. Admit your mistakes.

Prescribe

2. Offer suggestions that get right to the point.
10. Tell others clearly what you want from them.
18. Offer suggestions that build on others' ideas.
26. State your needs and expectations reasonably.
34. Keep others' attention on issues you feel are important.
42. Offer mutually beneficial exchanges and incentives.

Appreciate

3. Express your appreciation when others do something well.
11. Express your dissatisfaction when others don't do something well.
19. Tell others what you like about what they are doing.
27. Tell others what you don't like about what they are doing.

35. Gracefully accept feedback.
43. Apologise for your mistakes.

Inspire

4. Describe possibilities in ways that encourage others to share your enthusiasm and commitment.
12. Use metaphors, analogies, and vivid descriptions to heighten others' enthusiasm about possibilities.
20. Stress the importance of pulling together to achieve common goals.
28. Emphasise the values you have in common with others.
36. Talk from the heart about your values and ideals.
44. Encourage others to do more than they thought was possible.

Pull behaviours

Attend

5. Give others the time and attention they need to get their points across.
13. Pay careful attention without interrupting when others are trying to make their points.
21. Focus carefully on concerns that others express.
29. Back off if the timing is not right.
37. Face up to important issues.
45. Remain patient and receptive when others disagree with or challenge your point of view.

Ask

6. Ask others for the bases for their decisions.
14. Ask others for their suggestions.
22. Ask questions such as "Could you give me a few examples to help me understand?"
30. Ask questions like "How can I help?" "How can I support you?"
38. Focus on "What can we learn from this mistake?" not on "Who is to blame?"
46. Ask others directly about the effects your behaviour has on them.

Understand

7. Communicate your understanding by paraphrasing what others have said.
15. Act as a sounding board to help others clarify their thinking.
23. Summarise areas of agreement or mutual interest.
31. Try to clarify and explore points on which you differ or disagree with others.
39. Communicate your understanding through the tone of your voice.
47. Communicate your understanding in nonverbal ways.

Empathise

8. Communicate your understanding of how a situation makes others feel.
16. Help others to clarify their feelings.
24. Show your genuine desire to find out how others feel.
32. Support others when they are facing difficult situations.
40. Give others the confidence to disclose how they feel about themselves.
48. Empathise with others.

Bibliography

1. Riane Eisler, *The Chalice and The Blade: Our History and Our Future*, Harper & Row, 1987, New York.
2. Mitch Albom, *Tuesday's With Maurie*, New York, Doubleday, 1997.
3. William H. Hudson, *Far Away and Long Ago: A History of My Early Life*, AMS Press, 1986.
4. Leo Buscaglia, *Love*, Fawcett Crest, New York, 1972.
5. David Viscott, M.D., *How To Live With Another Person*, Pocket Books, New York, 1974.
6. Rabbi Paysach J. Krohn, *Along the Maggid's Journey*, Mesorah Publications, Ltd.
7. Felix Salten, *Bambi: A Life In The Woods*, Simon & Schuster, New York, 1928 [Bambi is a registered Disney trademark.]
8. For more detail on the process of giving and receiving win-win feedback, see Irwin Rubin and Thomas Campbell, *The ABCs of Effective Feedback: A Guide For Caring Professionals*, Jossey-Bass, San Francisco, 1998.
9. This and other one line quotes used periodically were gathered from a variety of sources such as: The Perpetual Calendar of Motivational Quotes, Daily Reflections by Touchstones, and A New Day by Bantam.
10. Leo Buscaglia, *Living, Loving & Learning*, (edited by Steven Short) Holt, Rinehart, & Winston, New York, 1982.
11. © Cole Porter Trust, 1929.
12. Personal Communication from Alf Cousins, (Adelaide, Australia).
13. For more information on specific tools available to enhance our ABCs see www.temenosinc.com/ and The Behavior Minder™.
14. Neale Donald Walsh, *Friendship With God*, New York, Putnam Publishing Group, 1999.
15. Touchstones.
16. Perpetual Calendar.
17. Salten; *op cit*.
18. J. Allen Boone, *Kinship With All Life*, San Francisco, Harper, 1976.